The
War in the Desert

The British
at War

General Editor:
Ludovic Kennedy

Roger Parkinson

The
War in the Desert

Book Club Associates   London

This edition published 1976 by
Book Club Associates
By arrangement with Granada Publishing Ltd

Printed in Great Britain by
William Clowes & Sons, Limited
London, Beccles and Colchester

Contents

Acknowledgements

The photographs and illustrations in this book are reproduced by kind permission of the following. Those on pages 8, 12, 13, 14, 15, 19, 23, 24, 25, 28, 29, 30, 33, 34, 36, 39, 40, 43, 45, 46, 48, 49, 50, 51, 52-3, 54, 58, 60, 65, 66, 68, 69, 70, 73, 74-5, 76, 78, 82, 84, 86, 88, 90-91, 93, 100, 102-3, 104, 106-7, 108, 112, 115, 116, 117, 119, 121, 122, 125, 127, 132, 134, 135, 136, 138, 140, 143, 149, 150-51, 155, 157, 164-5, 166-7, 169, 170, 172, 174, 175, 176-7, 181, 186, 190-91, 194 and 196, Imperial War Museum; pages 18 and 160, by courtesy of the Lieutenant-Colonel of the Welsh Guards; pages 158-9, by courtesy of the Lieutenant-Colonel of the Scots Guards. Illustration Research Service and Celia Dearing supplied the pictures. The maps were drawn by Bucken Ltd.

The publisher would also like to thank Colonel G.P.B. Roberts for permission to quote extracts from his journals and Leo Cooper, publisher, for permission to quote from *Diary of a Desert Rat* by R. L. Crimp.

Introduction

Few campaigns in the second world war hold as much fascination as the conflict in North Africa. Even today, more than thirty years later, the names of its leaders – Rommel, Wavell, Auchinleck, Alexander, Montgomery – still have a magic ring. In many ways the desert war was like the war at sea, with the desert vast and empty as the ocean, tanks in great numbers being manoeuvred like cruisers, and the flexibility of movement that sea warfare always has. And like the war at sea, the battles were fought apart from the political influences that coloured campaigns elsewhere; the desert's few civilians were neutral.

Because it was fought in this vacuum, the desert war was, as Rommel put it, 'a war without hatred'. General Ravenstein, one of his subordinates, called it 'a gentleman's war'. The troops on both sides respected each other and still do; they shared and suffered the same discomforts, the heat, the thirst, the dust, the flies; the same inhospitable terrain of sand and scrub and naked rock.

If there was one lesson of war the desert campaign emphasised, it was this; that to advance, however far, is profitless unless the ground gained can be consolidated, or the momentum sustained. Time and time again one side made huge advances, only to have to fall back later, owing to the difficulties of maintaining extended lines.

All this Roger Parkinson brings out admirably in this well-documented book, whose pace well matches many of the battles it describes. The photographs too, taken by brave war cameramen of both sides, show graphically what the desert war must have been like.

Ludovic Kennedy

Chapter 1

Battle Begins

At precisely 4.45 p.m. on 10 June 1940 the British Ambassador in Rome stood before an elegant desk in the Italian Foreign Ministry. Count Ciano, Mussolini's Foreign Minister, informed Sir Percy Loraine that the King of Italy would consider himself in a state of war with Britain as from midnight 11 June. In his diary, Ciano described the British diplomat's reaction as 'laconic and inscrutable. He received my communication without batting an eyelid or changing colour ...' The Italian Minister made no mention in his journal of Sir Percy's supposed exit-line: 'I have the honour to remind Your Excellency that England is not in the habit of losing her wars.' Mussolini appeared on the balcony of the sumptuous Palazzo Venezia to announce the news of war to an unresponsive Roman crowd; Ciano moaned: 'I am sad, very sad. The adventure begins. May God help Italy.'

The Italian declaration had been expected. Both sides had made their war preparations; within hours, Italy opened hostilities. The Chiefs of Staff in London were informed at 10 a.m. on the 11th: 'Malta was bombed at 05.00 hours today.' In the North African desert, British armoured cars were plunging forward towards the Italian positions on the border between Egypt and the enemy province of Cyrenaica in Libya. And on the night of the 11th the velvety desert dark was abruptly slashed by vivid tracer fire and sudden explosions, when British troops of the 11th Hussars ambushed a column of Italian lorries near Fort Capuzzo. The Desert War had begun. It would end thirty-five months later after a gigantic, convulsive conflict which swayed backwards and forwards across the North African wastelands, and which resulted in the opposing armies each advancing and retreating nearly four thousand miles in their attempts to annihilate the other.

Opposite British armoured units at Fort Capuzzo, scene of the first clash with Axis troops in the Desert War.

Rommel called the conflict a war without hatred – '*Krieg ohne Hass*'. General von Ravenstein, commander of the 21st Panzer Division, described it as a 'gentleman's war'. Winston Churchill risked criticism when he took the almost unprecedented step of praising an enemy commander during time of war: in January 1942 he paid tribute to Rommel in a speech to the Commons. 'We have a very daring and skilful opponent against us, and, may I say across the havoc of war, a great general.' After the guns had fallen silent men who had fought against each other in this unique and almost chivalrous conflict found themselves sharing a common bond. Ravenstein declared:

If the warriors of the Africa campaign meet today anywhere in the world, be they Englishmen or Scots, Germans or Italians, Indians, New

9

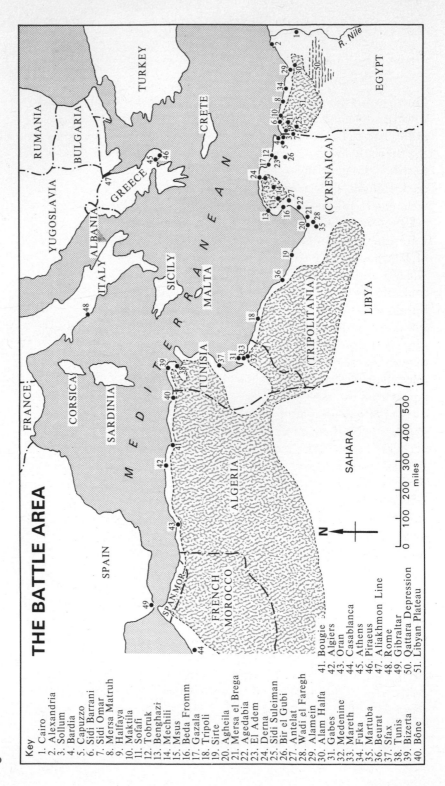

THE BATTLE AREA

Key
1. Cairo
2. Alexandria
3. Sollum
4. Bardia
5. Capuzzo
6. Sidi Barrani
7. Sidi Omar
8. Mersa Matruh
9. Halfaya
10. Maktila
11. Sofafi
12. Tobruk
13. Benghazi
14. Mechili
15. Msus
16. Beda Fromm
17. Gazala
18. Tripoli
19. Sirte
20. Agheila
21. Mersa el Brega
22. Agedabia
23. El Adem
24. Derna
25. Sidi Suleiman
26. Bir el Gubi
27. Antelat
28. Wadi el Faregh
29. Alamein
30. Alam Halfa
31. Gabes
32. Medenine
33. Mareth
34. Fuka
35. Martuba
36. Beurat
37. Sfax
38. Tunis
39. Bizerta
40. Bône
41. Bougie
42. Algiers
43. Oran
44. Casablanca
45. Athens
46. Piraeus
47. Aliakhmon Line
48. Rome
49. Gibraltar
50. Qattara Depression
51. Libyan Plateau

Zealanders or South Africans, they greet each other as staunch old comrades. It is an invisible but strong link which binds them all. The fight in Africa was fierce, but fair. They respected each other, and still do so today.

One reason for this strange, seemingly old-fashioned attitude towards the enemy stemmed from the battlefield itself. All nationalities had to live and fight under the tough conditions imposed by the weird wilderness, constantly changing yet always potentially hostile – the fierce heat and biting cold, the gritty sand, fine sand, dark shingle, flint, hard-baked mud, limestone, gravel. The unwelcome terrain covered the whole of the principal campaign area – Egypt in the east, bordering onto Cyrenaica, then Tripolitania. Later the war would extend from Tripolitania into the mountains of Tunisia, and, on the other side of the theatre of war, into French Algeria and neighbouring Morocco. The most important fighting took place on and near the Egyptian and Libyan plateau, five hundred feet high, bordered by the Mediterranean coastal strip to the north and the Sahara in the south. The northern edge of the plateau drops steeply to the narrow coastal area, and the few passes down this escarpment therefore become of vital military importance. Desert conditions in turn resulted in a new type of warfare. Apart from the coastal road there existed few recognised routes, but on the plateau itself tanks and trucks could motor almost anywhere. War therefore became extremely mobile, almost naval: armoured cars acted as scouting destroyers, while the guns and tanks became battleships and cruisers. Campaigns flowed fast once they began to move, with armies covering vast distances. Territory proved to be largely unimportant: victory did not go to the side which controlled the largest area – the desert, like the sea, was worthless on its own. Indeed, the more desert held by one side, the greater that side's supply difficulties.

Both sides shared the same experiences – the same difficulties of supply, the same need to exploit mobility. They fought in an area isolated from major civilian centres. Like naval forces, or fighter pilots, men in the desert armies could concentrate on the purely military aspect of war: the desert conflict remained largely divorced from those political or ideological influences which polluted the campaign in Russia or in Europe in the closing stages of hostilities. But the same principle of war existed: kill or be killed. And, in those first days of desert war in June 1940, Britain desperately needed a victory.

Operation 'Dynamo', the evacuation of allied troops from Dunkirk, had been officially declared finished by the Admiralty only   11

Part of the notorious
Halfaya – 'Hellfire' –
pass, through which ran
one of the few vital
roads from the Libyan
plateau to the coastal
area.

seven days before. About 338,226 troops had been rescued, of whom
225,000 were British; they had brought back little more than rifles,
bayonets and a few machine-guns. Among the last to leave had been
General Harold Alexander, commanding the rearguard; later he
would win fame in the desert. Meanwhile Britain seemed virtually
defenceless against invasion; France would survive only until 21
June. For months the Germans would be able to enjoy the initiative,
throwing the *Luftwaffe* against the British fighter pilots during this
'Spitfire Summer', organising the bomber force for the Blitz, and
stabbing at Britain's sea-links across the Atlantic. Only in faraway
North Africa could the British army hope to attack with any chance
of success.

But the task would be tremendous. General Sir Archibald
Wavell, who had taken up his appointment as British commander
on 2 August 1939, had a huge command area which symbolised the
stretched British situation. He exercised general control over all
British land forces in Egypt, the Sudan, Palestine and Transjordan,
Cyprus, British Somaliland, Aden, Iraq and the shores of the Per-
sian Gulf. British forces had to be scattered far and wide – and these
units were anyway deficient following the need to build up maximum defences in Britain herself. On 11 June 1940, Wavell had
about thirty-six thousand men in Egypt, but equipment remained
in short supply. The 7th Armoured Division had only four regiments of tanks; the 4th Indian Division was short of artillery and an
entire brigade; the New Zealand Division only amounted to one

Indian troops on board their carrier – one of the many different nationalities included in the desert armies.

brigade group. About twenty-seven thousand British troops were stationed in Palestine, and East African countries remained even more lightly garrisoned. British forces in North Africa were vastly outnumbered: Marshal Graziani, the Italian commander, had about one million men in Cyrenaica and Tripolitania, while the Duke of Aosta commanded nearly 300,000 Italians in Mussolini's East African territory. Lack of equipment and fully trained formations worried Wavell more than disparity in numbers of men; nevertheless, he planned to attack.

On 8 June General Richard O'Connor, who enjoyed a reputation for boldness and vigorous originality, had been given command of all forces in the Western Desert, subordinate to Wavell. He had orders to take offensive action against the Italians at the Egyptian frontier immediately war was declared; three days later his forces stabbed forward. Almost before some of the enemy soldiers realised they were at war, their frontier positions were under assault. The ambush undertaken by the 11th Hussars on the first night of conflict revealed the Italians to be unprepared; O'Connor, living up to his reputation, ordered strikes to be made at Forts

13

Drawing of General Sir
Archibald Wavell, by
Rosciwensky (Tom
Titt).

Maddalena and Capuzzo. The first surrendered next day, after
A Squadron, 11th Hussars, had driven their armoured cars across
fifty miles of open desert. Fort Capuzzo also fell. On 22 June Wavell
could signal London: 'At small cost we have inflicted casualties
wherever enemy forces encountered, capturing twenty-five Italian

officers and five hundred ORs ... Early attacks completely surprised enemy ... Morale of all ranks admirable.' Operations in Libya and in East and Equatorial Africa had revealed the 'superiority, initiative, skill and daring of our forward troops'. The news proved intensely welcome in the London gloom. General Sir John Dill, Chief of the Imperial General Staff, replied: 'All these operations are of immense value at this time and publicity of your remarkable local successes has also importance.'

Mechanics undertake urgent repairs on tanks in the forward area; behind them are the mobile recovery vehicles, well spread out to prevent a target being presented for enemy aircraft.

But Wavell's successes could only be limited. By the end of July about two hundred tanks were under repair, from the Western Desert Force's normal complement of 306. The sixty miles of frontier between Sollum and Fort Maddalena had to be covered by an extremely thin screen, backed by formations of dummy tanks, while almost every tracked vehicle in the forward area was ordered into workshops for overhaul and refit. Men were as weary as their machines, though they continued to harass and worry the Italians with the few vehicles at their disposal. At the close of June Wavell had established the Long Range Desert Group, which soon became expert at using the desert to best advantage. Yet enterprise, daring and initiative would be insufficient: the British had morale and ascendancy, but the Italians still had far greater numerical strength. Wavell remained under intense pressure from his widely scattered commitments; in London, Winston Churchill began to interfere in the commander's fragile dispersion of forces, seeking more action and victories to boost the battered morale at home.

By early August the Italians had massed the equivalent of an army corps in Ethiopia and were beginning to advance against

15

isolated British Somaliland; already, on 15 July, the Italian Supreme Command had ordered Rudolfo Graziani to be prepared to launch an offensive against Egypt, despite Graziani's own reluctance for such a venture. Eight days later a depressing signal reached London from Wavell, warning that unless critical shortages could be made up within three months, his army's position would be at risk. Churchill reacted with an explosive minute to the Chiefs of Staff: 'What is happening to the concert of the campaign in the Middle East?' He became increasingly critical of Wavell, whom he had never met, and explanations put forward by the Chiefs of Staff and Anthony Eden, then War Secretary, failed to satisfy him. 'Dined with Winston,' noted Eden in his diary on 25 July. 'Violent tirade after about Middle East and Wavell and at times heated altercation.'

Another anxious telegram arrived from Cairo on the 30th: 'We cannot continue indefinitely to fight this war without proper equipment and I hope the Middle East requirements will be delayed no longer.' Wavell received a summons to return to London for talks; on the evening of 7 August he reported at the War Office and early next morning talked alone with Eden, with the War Secretary describing him afterwards as 'in good heart, but the deficiencies are shocking'. Wavell then outlined the situation to the Chiefs of Staff: pressure against British Somaliland; limited Italian gains on the Kenya–Abyssinia border; Italian numerical superiority in the Western Desert. The real desert danger, he claimed, would be the introduction of German armoured and motorised units, and he warned that owing to lack of pre-war preparations, British intelligence sources in Libya were deficient – German troops might therefore arrive without immediate British knowledge. Wavell would have been slightly reassured if he could have overheard a discussion in Rome on this same day, Thursday 8 August, between Ciano and Graziani. The army commander informed the Italian Foreign Minister that the proposed attack on Egypt was 'a very serious undertaking … Our present preparations are far from perfect.' Graziani added: 'We move towards a defeat which, in the desert, must inevitably develop into a rapid and total disaster.'

Also on 8 August Wavell had his first meeting with Churchill. From the start the two men failed to establish a satisfactory relationship. The politician and soldier were in many ways complete contrasts: Churchill was ebullient, Wavell taciturn; Churchill always seemed optimistic, while Wavell displayed caution. The General failed to respond to the Prime Minister's emotional oratory. Churchill insisted on intervening in matters of troop dispositions,

16

and wanted South African and West African troops shifted from East Africa to Egypt or the Sudan; Wavell resented this intervention, and anyway doubted the wisdom of such a transfer. 'I am pretty sure,' wrote Wavell later, 'that he considered my replacement by someone who was more likely to share his ideas, but could not find any good reason to do so. Winston has always disliked me personally.' The two men clashed on the subject of the route to be taken by convoy reinforcements to the Middle East, with the Prime Minister wanting to rush them through the dangerous Mediterranean and Wavell – despite the urgency – advising that they should go the safer although longer route round the Cape. The matter had still to be settled when Wavell left London on the evening of 15 August. He arrived in Cairo twenty-four hours later. During his absence the Italians had attacked in British Somaliland and the last British troops were evacuated on the 18th.

Churchill lost his bid to have the convoy go through the Mediterranean. No signs could be seen of imminent enemy activity in Libya, and time could therefore perhaps just be spared for the longer route to be used; the supplies of tanks, guns and spare parts began to arrive up the Suez Canal on 5 September. Meanwhile the Italian commander had continued to hesitate: on 29 August Mussolini himself had told Graziani to launch an attack from Libya by 10 September; Graziani continued to delay; on 7 September the Duce demanded an attack in two days' time. Graziani reluctantly gave the necessary orders. The 10th Italian Army under Berti, with the 12th and 13th Corps, would advance along the coast road and attack Sidi Barrani. 'Never,' wrote Count Ciano, 'has a military operation been undertaken so much against the will of the commander.' And yet the Italians would total five divisions, against which the British could only deploy a thin defensive screen.

The Italian offensive began on 13 September, after a further delay caused by units losing their way to their assembly point at Sidi Omar, and after renewed anxiety felt by Graziani when he received reports of 'massive British armoured forces' gathering to oppose him. Wavell, in fact, planned no serious opposition on the frontier.

> My plan for the defence of Egypt was to await the invaders at the defence of Matruh, and counter-attack them there. If they by-passed the Matruh defences and pushed on towards the Delta, I had had further defences prepared ... covering their chief supplies of water.

British forces therefore withdrew to Matruh; the Italians quickly occupied Sollum and pushed on to take the Halfaya Pass on the 15th. At 6.30 a.m. on the 15th a mobile force advanced towards   17

The ideal kit lay-out, as depicted by Rex Whistler – an example of the kind of 'bull' usually abandoned in the enforced informality of desert fighting.

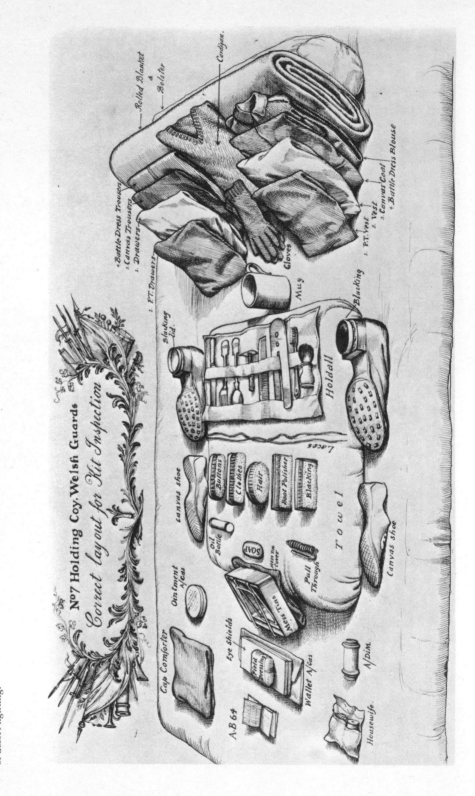

Sidi Barrani, entering this dirty ramshackle collection of mud huts at 3.30 p.m. on the 16th. A farcical communiqué issued in Rome declared: 'All is quiet and the trams are again running in the town of Sidi Barrani.' Graziani, content with his cautious, unopposed advance sixty miles into Egypt, began to dig in. Wavell expressed himself well satisfied: 'The withdrawal of our small force was effected with admirable skill, and there is no doubt whatever that very serious losses were inflicted on the enemy ... Our own losses were under fifty men and a small number of vehicles.' Already, two days before the Italian move had started, Wavell had sent a note to his Chief of Staff, requesting a study to be made of a British offensive into Cyrenaica. 'We may ... hope to be dealing with a somewhat dispirited and not very formidable Italian, and to be able to take a certain degree of risk.' Wavell's assessment of his enemy seemed confirmed by Ciano's diary entry for 2 October: 'Graziani insists that we shall have to wait quite a long time, at least until the end of November, in order to complete preparations [for renewed advance].' Wavell intensified his plans to attack before Graziani could gather his strength again – and before the Germans arrived to succour their ally.

Meanwhile, troops in the desert had settled down to the daily routine which would become increasingly familiar. Men of the 7th Armoured Division, the original soldiers to be called by the famous nickname of Desert Rats, had learnt to live with and use the desert, rather than to fear their strange environment.

A desert bivouac, sketched on the spot by T. White. Stoves were improvised; men used their trenches for beds; tents were needed to keep out the cold night air.

Life here is one hundred per cent open-air under the broiling sun by day, [wrote one private, R. L. Crimp] and by night in blanket-beds

19

made up on the hard desert surface, under the stars. The focal point in the section area is the section-truck, with all its gear now unloaded around it 'to ease the springs'. Nearby is the 'kitchen', a couple of fire-places built of cut-down petrol-cans on the ground ... Everything is absolutely austere and primitive.

Daily life focused on the section-truck, battered and sand-stained.

All our gear and supplies have to go on board: each man's rifle and the section weapons ... a large Italian medical chest, picked up on a pre-vious campaign, now used as the section box in which is kept our current supply of rations; another box containing the section reserve of tinned food, only to be used in an emergency; and yet another recept-acle for storing our feeding utensils ... Then there are about half a dozen two-gallon water-cans for daily use, and an equal number carried full as another 'untouchable' reserve; then the driver's tool-box, a spare wheel, and several spades. On top of this lot, everyone has to find room for his large pack, haversack, webbing equipment, overcoat and bed-ding roll; also gas-mask and hat ...

No matter how adept the troops were at desert existence, some aspects would always remain almost intolerable – especially the flies.

Soon after sunrise they arrive in hordes from nowhere, then plague us with malign persistence all through the day, swarming and buzzing around, trying desperately to land on our faces, in our eyes, ears and nostrils, on our arms, hands, knees, and necks. And once settled, they bite hard. Desert sores, oases of succulence, draw them like magnets. In fact everything unwholesome, filthy and putrefied is manna to them.

These forward units, later to become the British 8th Army, were still far too few on the ground; and they still lacked essential equip-ment. Wavell, hoping to seize the initiative, could only plan for a raid upon the Italian positions rather than a full-scale offensive. And now came a further complication. Mussolini made another bid for military glory, this time in south-east Europe. At 3 a.m. on 28 October Italy delivered an ultimatum to Greece, which the Greeks immediately rejected. Within hours Italy launched a major offen-sive on the country via Albania, and the Greeks had already asked Britain for military help in the event of such an assault. This assist-ance could only come from British forces in the Middle East. Eden was in Cairo at this time, consulting with Wavell; during the even-ing of 2 November he received a telegram from Churchill: 'Greek situation must be held to dominate others now.' Eden impatiently scribbled across this cable: 'Egypt more important than Greece.' The War Secretary had been told by Wavell of plans for an early British offensive against the Italians in the Western Desert; with-drawal of strength at this stage would be disastrous. Churchill on

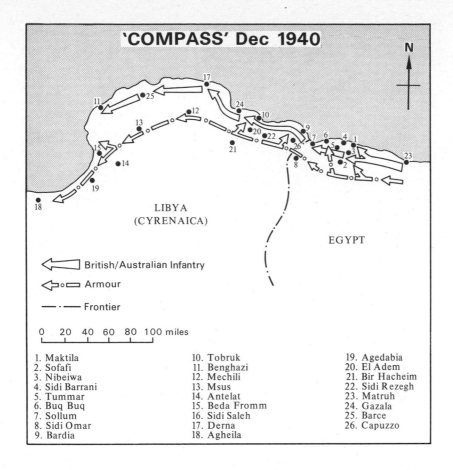

'COMPASS' Dec 1940

N

LIBYA
(CYRENAICA)

EGYPT

◁▭ British/Australian Infantry

◁–o▭ Armour

—·— Frontier

0 20 40 60 80 100 miles

1. Maktila	10. Tobruk	19. Agedabia
2. Sofafi	11. Benghazi	20. El Adem
3. Nibeiwa	12. Mechili	21. Bir Hacheim
4. Sidi Barrani	13. Msus	22. Sidi Rezegh
5. Tummar	14. Antelat	23. Matruh
6. Buq Buq	15. Beda Fromm	24. Gazala
7. Sollum	16. Sidi Saleh	25. Barce
8. Sidi Omar	17. Derna	26. Capuzzo
9. Bardia	18. Agheila	

the other hand believed Wavell merely intended to remain on the
defensive, hoarding troops and equipment while Greece suffered.
Eden returned home on the 8th; he immediately saw Dill, then
hurried to Churchill's underground rooms near Piccadilly where
he described Wavell's plans. Within minutes the Prime Minister
'purred like six cats'. Churchill's reaction was typical: all possible
support should now be given for the enterprise, despite other commitments, and the operations must be considered top priority. Yet
Wavell had been anxious to avoid such over-enthusiasm – he had
only disclosed his plans to Eden to prevent strength being taken
from him for Greece – and he knew the way would now be open for
pressure from Churchill for premature action. Sure enough, the
Prime Minister sent a cable to Wavell on 14 November which
declared: 'It seems that now is the time to take risks and strike.'
Wavell chose to send his reply, dated the 16th, to Eden rather than
Churchill, and he refused to be hurried. 'Operation is in preparation but not possible to execute this month as originally hoped. Now

working to date about end first week December unless enemy moves meanwhile.'

The days seemed to drag for Churchill, so desperate for a morale-boosting victory. He anxiously awaited news of the desert operation, code-named 'Compass'; he had been excited by Wavell's plans, and now the waiting, which Eden found 'uneasy', was to Churchill becoming intolerable. The War Secretary argued against additional pressure, but a further appeal for action reached Cairo on the 20th; two days later Churchill sent an angry minute to the War Secretary: 'Every day's delay endangers secrecy in Egypt, which must be full of Italian spies and agents.' Wavell received another exhortation from the Prime Minister on the 26th: 'News from every quarter must have impressed on you the importance of "Compass" in relation to whole Middle East position ...' Further signals in the first days of December demanded to know the date for the operations; Wavell obliged on the 6th: 'If weather permits preliminary move night 7/8 December, approach march night 8/9 December, attack morning 9 December.' But the next paragraph raised renewed anger at Ten Downing Street. 'Feel undue hopes being placed on this operation which was designed as raid only. We are greatly outnumbered on ground and in air, have to move seventy-five miles over desert and attack enemy who has fortified himself for three months.' Churchill expressed his 'shock' and declared: 'If, with the situation as it is, General Wavell is only playing small, and is not hurling on his whole available force with furious energy, he will have failed to rise to the heights of circumstances.'

Wavell calmly completed his plans. The enemy held a series of fortified camps from Maktila on the coast stretching fifty miles inland to Sofafi, above the escarpment. Behind this line enemy forces had been deployed in depth, but the forward camps were not mutually supporting: a wide gap existed between Sofafi and the nearest group at Nibeiwa. O'Connor would therefore strike through this gap, masking Sofafi while he surged north to the coast and rolled up the other positions. The stab through the gap would be launched during the night. Plans for a desert offensive were virtually impossible to keep totally hidden, and to reach the Italian positions the British would have to make a long and vulnerable approach over the open desert. O'Connor carefully deployed his forces. The main assault would be launched by the 4th Indian Division; the pursuit force would consist of the 7th Armoured. On the coast, a mixed group known as Selby Force and aided by dummy tanks would hold the Italian division at Maktila. Total

British strength numbered thirty-six thousand; enemy strength would be about four times greater.

Wavell spent the afternoon of Saturday, 7 December, at the horse-races in Cairo; during the evening he gave a dinner at the Turf Club. Meanwhile the British assault forces were slipping forward over the open desert. In Rome, Ciano recorded in his diary on the 8th: 'Nothing new.' But by nightfall on the 8th both the 7th Armoured and 4th Indian divisions had reached their assembly points in the approaches to the gap between enemy positions at Sofafi and Nibeiwa. Men shivered in the bitter cold as they awaited dawn. In the centre, Matilda tanks and troops from the 11th Indian Infantry Brigade moved thirteen miles to their final positions for the Nibeiwa attack. Bombing raids by the Desert Air Force and naval bombardment of Sidi Barrani and Maktila helped conceal this last deployment, and, at 4.45 a.m. on Monday, 9 December, infantry fire opened up on the east of Nibeiwa to attract enemy attention to that area. At 7 a.m. the seventy-two guns of the divisional artillery began a brief bombardment, also to the east; ten minutes later infantry tanks of the 7th Royal Tank Regiment crashed into Nibeiwa from the north-west. Twenty-three Italian medium and light tanks parked outside the camp were destroyed; British armour swept into the enemy positions. Two battalions of British infantry

A dead Italian lies beside his anti-tank gun, killed in the vicious and sudden British offensive.

23

rushed in behind the tanks, and within two hours the camp had been taken. The tanks squealed northwards to the next objective, Tummar. On the left, 7th Armoured Division had moved at first light, covering Sofafi and driving north through the gap to cut the road east of Buq Buq. On the right, Selby Force proved insufficient to prevent Italians withdrawing from Maktila to protect Sidi Barrani, but the twin drives north by the 7th Armoured and 4th Indian divisions threatened to surround this retreating enemy army.

Churchill fretted for fresh news. He learnt on the 10th that a second push forward had been made by the 7th Armoured Division and large numbers of prisoners had been taken – too many to count but amounting to 'about five acres of officers and two hundred acres of other ranks'. The Prime Minister beamed at one message relayed to London from a young tank officer: 'Have arrived at the second B in Buq Buq.' Sidi Barrani fell during the evening. The enemy continued to fall back, although offering fierce resistance in isolated

pockets; on 12 December the British armoured units leapt forward again. But also on the 12th Wavell decided he must now withdraw the 4th Indian Division from the battle to be sent immediately to the Sudan for operations against the Italians at Kassala. Wavell told London that he had ordered O'Connor to continue the advance as best he could. 'Mobile column of Armoured Division will advance to Sollum–Capuzzo and endeavour to get across Tobruk road and cut off Bardia. If Bardia falls, though I think this unlikely, I have instructed O'Connor that he can push on towards Tobruk up to the limit of endurance of vehicles and men.'

British guns and equipment pass through Sidi Barrani as Wavell's advance sweeps forward.

In three days, from dawn on the 9th to evening on the 11th, O'Connor's 'raid' had captured nearly 40,000 Italian and Libyan prisoners, 237 guns and 73 light and medium tanks. British losses had been 624 killed, wounded and missing. Withdrawing units of the 4th Indian Division were replaced as they left by regiments of the 6th Australian Division, thus maintaining British strength, but the administrative problems surrounding these transfers of men and material inevitably slowed down the advance and delayed final victory. Nevertheless by the evening of the 12th the only Italians left in Egypt were those blocking the approach to Sollum and scattered remnants around Sidi Omar; two days later most of the Armoured Division had crossed the frontier into Libya, although less than half of its tanks remained fit for action after suffering countless mechanical breakdowns. Bardia, the next objective, loomed ahead.

Both sides prepared for the struggle for this important port. General 'Electric Whiskers' Bergonzoli, commander of the Italian 23rd Corps, was confident of his ability to hold his Bardia position: Mussolini had been informed that the troops would fight to the end. Garrisons from Sollum and Capuzzo had been gathered in to   25 strengthen defences, and Bergonzoli now had the equivalent of four divisions totalling forty-five thousand men and four hundred guns behind an eighteen-mile defensive perimeter. Wavell, who flew up to the desert early on the 16th, under-estimated enemy strength by more than a half. Timing for an assault had to be delayed for about two weeks, while the 4th Indian–6th Australian transfer was completed, and meanwhile the battered 7th Armoured units ringed the northern edge of the enemy positions – leaving a loophole in the hope that the enemy would retreat along the road to Tobruk, where they could be caught out in the open. Wavell reported to London on the 19th: 'Hunt is still going but first racing burst over, hounds brought to their noses, huntsmen must cast and second horses badly needed. It may be necessary to dig this fox.' The General spent Christmas checking the arms situation: 7th Armoured now had nearly seventy cruiser and 120 light tanks in action, but only twenty-five infantry tanks were available and all were badly in need of repair; not more than eighteen could be expected to take part in the attack on Bardia. Churchill, still pressing for maximum effort in minimum time, spared a few hours of Christmas relaxation at his Chequers retreat; Mussolini stayed in sleety, miserable Rome, where Ciano noted: 'The Duce is sombre.'

The year ended with rumblings of renewed conflict in Albania, where the Greeks had continued to hold the Italians. Hitler might soon send help – and this might affect British strength in North Africa through the need to send aid to Greece. Churchill told the Defence Committee of the War Cabinet early in January that 'there was little doubt that the Germans were collecting a considerable force in Roumania and would be ready to move an army on any date after 20 January ... We must, therefore, do our utmost to assist the Greeks ... even at the expense of further advance into Libya.' He added: 'It is now necessary to decide how much further we should advance in Libya. The fine port of Benghazi was a tempting objective. We might, however, have to rest content with Tobruk.' First, Bardia would have to be taken. And, in the early hours of 3 January, the attack began, spearheaded by Australian troops, who now received their first blooding in the Second World War – and who would soon become famous among desert fighters.

From the start the Australians displayed dash and daring. Infantry units moved forward while strong artillery support battered enemy positions on the perimeter wire. By the first pink tinge of dawn two lanes had been cleared through the anti-tank ditch, the wire and the minefield in the eastern defensive sector; Australian infantrymen clung to the outlying Italian positions and behind them the tanks screeched through the smoke to pass through the gap. Fanning out behind the defences, the tanks plunged into the Italians while a massive bombardment from three battleships shook the northern sector. By noon the enemy were surrendering in scores, although individual pockets continued to fight bravely. After forty-eight hours of mopping up the fortress had surrendered, and 45,000 prisoners and 462 guns fell into British hands. Australian casualties totalled 456.

Already, on the day of victory, Wavell had issued orders for plans to be prepared for a further advance with Benghazi the final objective; O'Connor's tanks were pushing forward for Tobruk. Churchill, in his congratulatory cable to Wavell in Cairo, warned: 'Time is short. I cannot believe that Hitler will not intervene soon ...' Yet next day, 7 January, the War Cabinet discussed the possibility of sending more help to Greece – at the expense of North Africa. Ministers were told that allied advance elements were already westward of Tobruk and the fall of the fortress seemed a certainty; operations in the last month had accounted for a third of the total Italian strength in Libya. Churchill then said he had asked the Chiefs of Staff to consider 'whether we could now afford some further assistance to Greece' in view of the perilous situation in that country, and Ministers agreed the subject should receive further consideration. Forty-eight hours later, on the 9th, the Defence Committee decided the first priority should be the capture of Tobruk, but after this Libyan operations should be severely limited and assistance to Greece would assume paramount importance.

The Chiefs of Staff told Cairo that the Government were prepared to authorise the despatch to Greece of mechanised and specialised units, plus air forces, to the limits of one infantry tank squadron, one cruiser regiment, ten artillery regiments and five aircraft squadrons. A worried reply reached London from Wavell on the 10th: the message from the Chiefs of Staff 'fills us with dismay', and Wavell and his colleagues warned that German moves in the Balkans might be a bluff, 'with the object of helping Italy by upsetting Greek nerves, inducing us to disperse our forces in the Middle East and to stop our advance in Libya'. Nothing could be sent from North Africa sufficient to stop the German advance into Greece, and to disperse the desert forces would be 'playing the enemy's game'. Within two hours after receiving this reply, Churchill sent another cable to Cairo.

Our information contradicts idea that German concentration in Roumania is merely 'move in war of nerves' or 'bluff to cause dispersion of forces' ... Destruction of Greece would eclipse victories you have

Australians advance
under the cover of a
dense smoke screen.

gained in Libya … Nothing must hamper capture of Tobruk but thereafter all operations in Libya are subordinated to aiding Greece … We
expect and require prompt and active compliance with our decisions.

Wavell had already suggested he should go to Athens to examine
the situation for himself; Churchill now said this visit 'should not
be delayed'.

Complete divergence of opinion therefore existed. Churchill
believed the next German move would come through the Balkans;
Wavell urged that British success in North Africa be consolidated
before the Germans intervened in the desert. Both the Prime
Minister and the General were correct. Next day, 11 January,
Hitler issued his War Directive No. 22. 'The situation in the Mediterranean area, where England is employing superior forces against
our allies, requires that Germany should assist.' German units
would start to move to Libya on about 20 January; *Luftwaffe* squadrons, in addition to flying from Sicily, would operate from airfields
28   in Tripoli in direct support of Italian land forces in the desert. But

the Führer also declared: 'German formations in the approximate strength of one Corps … will be detailed and made ready to move to Albania.'

Wavell flew to Athens on Monday, 13 January, and immediately found another tangle in the complicated military and diplomatic threads. The official Greek position differed completely from the British assessment. General Ioannis Metaxas, President of the Greek Council, believed British troops offered for the defence of northern Greece would be insufficient and would merely provoke German attack; General Alexander Papagos, the army chief, declined the artillery and tanks offered for the Albanian front and sought transport and clothing instead. The Defence Committee considered the surprising Greek reaction at a meeting on the evening of the 16th, and could only conclude that if the Greeks refused to accept help, British emphasis should once again shift back to North Africa. The confusion affected planning for the desert campaign; Wavell told Dill on the 18th that he would continue to plan for an advance to Benghazi, but he warned that the existing proposal to send help to Greece was a 'dangerous half-measure … We shall almost inevitably be compelled to send further troops in haste or shall become involved in retreat or defeat. Meanwhile advance into Libya will be halted and Italians given time to recover.'

General Ioannis Metaxas, Prime Minister of Greece.

During this wrangle the troops in the desert had continued to exert pressure on Tobruk. Activity had been constant in the scorching sun: ammunition had been dragged up, gun emplacements carved from the scrub, engineers had toiled over the tanks night and day to make them ready for battle. A vicious sandstorm on the 20th delayed the moment for attack, but men struggled with their final preparations as the grit-laden wind lashed their faces. At 8.30 a.m. on 21 January the assault went in. O'Connor intended to use the same methods which had proved so successful at Bardia. Australian infantrymen swarmed forward in the south-east sector; infantry tanks rumbled at their heels, passed through, and spread out inside the perimeter wire under cover of a slamming artillery barrage. By midday the 16th Australian Brigade and the 19th Brigade had reached their objectives, but Italian opposition stiffened as coastal and AA guns were brought round into action against the attackers. British units edged forward until by flickering nightfall they were ranged along the escarpment overlooking Tobruk town itself; throughout darkness they continued to fight forward, while Italians in Tobruk prepared to surrender. Fires flared in the houses; the air shook with rumbling explosions; acrid smoke swept upwards to the attackers' positions.

29

British troops rise from cover to advance on Tobruk.

At dawn on 22 January the final attack began, to meet virtually no resistance, and the last stronghold fell during the early afternoon. Nearly 30,000 prisoners were taken, plus 236 guns and 87 tanks – and so many vehicles that no one could be bothered to count them. The Western Desert Force, now called the 13th Corps, had suffered just over four hundred casualties. Morale among the Australian and British troops soared high. The road lay open before them. And following the Greek reluctance to accept aid and the consequent shift of priority back to North Africa, the Chiefs of Staff had cabled Wavell on 21 January, the day of the attack on Tobruk, to say Benghazi should be the next target. Capture of this port might mean the virtual end of the Italian army in North Africa as an effective fighting force. Churchill signalled enthusiastic praise on the 23rd: 'The daring and scope of the original conception, the perfection of staff work and execution have raised the reputation of the British and Australian Army and its leadership, and will long be regarded as models of the military art ...' But two days earlier, even before Tobruk had fallen, Hitler and Mussolini had been closeted in the Führer's HQ in the mountains at Berghof: German help to the Italians in North Africa, operation 'Sunflower', would be accelerated – including the despatch of the 5th Light (Motorised) Division on about 15 February.

Moreover, the next stage in the British advance raised new difficulties. Capture of Benghazi entailed the conquest of the whole Cyrenaica bulge, and this area favoured defence rather than offensive operations: open desert and scrubland changed to a region of rough hills and valleys which hindered movement. The main coastal road offered the best line of advance, but would obviously be heavily defended; secondary roads were poor, while further south the absence of communication links led the Italians to believe the going would be impossible for large forces. Climatic conditions over the whole bulge provided a further drawback, with frequent rain bogging the roads. In addition, the British units were now operating at the end of a long supply line, and many vehicles needed urgent overhaul.

Thus on 26 January, after a clash near Mechili, the 4th Armoured Brigade were unable to pursue retreating Italian forces because of mechanical troubles, rain, and shortages of petrol. O'Connor refused to be deterred. He planned a bold operation – the first great left hook of the North African battles. While the Australians continued to push along the main coastal road, the expected line of advance, another strike forward would be made across the 'impassable' wilderness further south, using the 7th Armoured Division. This southern hook would advance via Mechili, Msus and Antelat to Beda Fromm and Sidi Saleh to cut the road to Tripoli: the retreating Italian army moving from Benghazi would therefore be trapped between the encircling 7th Armoured and the Australians. Wavell approved the plan on 1 February. In view of the maintenance difficulties and vehicle deficiencies, it seemed advisable to await the arrival at the front of two more armoured regiments, expected about 7 February, but reports reaching O'Connor late on the 2nd seemed to confirm an Italian withdrawal. No time could be lost if the enemy army was to be intercepted. The 11th Hussars, leading the 7th Armoured Division's left hook, received orders to advance.

The movement proved among the most brilliant and courageous of the whole desert war. Armoured cars had to move into unknown and forbidding terrain; Colonel John Combe, commanding the 11th Hussars with 2nd Rifle Brigade and three artillery batteries, even lacked adequate maps. The leading units left Mechili at first light on 4 February, and the first fifty miles were indeed terrible: troops swore and sweated as they hauled their vehicles over the rock and steep slopes; engines overheated and spluttered to a stop and were nursed forward again. By daybreak on the 5th the British had reached a point east of Msus, but reports from further north revealed an even faster Italian withdrawal than expected, and Colonel Combe had to hurry his units onwards at increased pace. By 12.30 p.m. on the 5th the 11th Hussars, Rifle Brigade and the guns of the Royal Horse Artillery had broken from the rough ground and were astride the main road near Beda Fromm before the Italians arrived. Within two hours leading elements of the enemy garrison retreating from Benghazi came in sight down the shimmering road. Combe had less than two thousand men and no tanks; the Benghazi garrison would total about twenty thousand with plentiful armour. But the British had the advantage of surprise. Guns, suddenly roaring from the hillsides, threw the enemy into confusion, and the Rifle Brigade blocking the main road hurled back Italian attempts to break through; C Squadron of the 11th Hussars wheeled their armoured cars south to prevent an out-flanking movement. For three hours the thin British line held. Then, in the early evening, Combe received news of the imminent arrival of reinforcements – leading tanks of the 4th Armoured Brigade advancing in front of the remainder of the 7th Armoured Division. These tanks, six cruisers and some light tanks from the 7th Hussars, appeared to the left and rear of the Italian column now stationary ten miles north of the Rifle Brigade position; their commanding officer spared no time for complicated orders, and merely snapped one word of command over the crackling radio. 'Attack!' In swooped this tiny British force with guns blazing, to create panic amongst the thousands of Italians. Fire swept through the vehicles; hundreds of Italians came running forward to surrender – providing an additional problem for the attackers. Only nightfall pre-vented full advantage being taken, and during the hours of darkness Italian strength steadily grew.

Battle became more intense next day, 6 February, spread along fifteen miles of road west of Beda Fromm. Time and again the enemy tried to break through the 7th Armoured Division, now reinforced by the later arrivals; scores of tanks lay burning along the road with oily black smoke gushing from the wreckage. Night fell again. The Rifle Brigade in Combe's force, still wedged across the main road, had to repel nine attempts to batter through. At dawn on the 7th the Italians gathered all their remaining tanks, about thirty, and made one last effort. Tanks followed by lorries broke through the leading Rifle Brigade companies, and the enemy infantry pushed forward into the bedlam of whining vehicles, clattering rifle-fire and thudding artillery. But one by one the enemy tanks were knocked out; the lines of infantry advancing against the British were held and then thrown back. Dirty white flags flapped from the Italian positions, and by 9 a.m. the battle had finished. Only fifteen miles away were the leading units from the Australian regiments pressing down the main coastal road from Benghazi in the Italian rear.

Triumph seemed total. O'Connor later reported: 'I think this may be termed a complete victory as none of the enemy escaped.' Less than two months had passed since Wavell had warned London: 'It may be necessary to dig this fox', and now O'Connor signalled

Damage to houses in
Benghazi by Italian
bombers after the British
occupation.

Cairo: 'Fox killed in the open.' Herds of prisoners had been taken,
estimated at 25,000, and 101 enemy tanks had been destroyed. 'We
came upon the scene of the campaign's last great battle,' wrote an
officer in the King's Royal Rifles, 'an imposing mess of shattered
Italian tanks, abandoned guns and derelict lorries.' Among the
captives were the mortally wounded army commander, General
Tellera, together with Bergonzoli and the entire Army HQ. In two
months two British divisions had advanced five hundred miles,
routing an army of ten divisions; total British and Australian
casualties numbered 2,000, but 130,000 enemy soldiers had been   33

General Sir John Dill and Anthony Eden.

captured, and nearly 400 tanks and over 800 guns had been taken or destroyed. The Desert Air Force had established complete supremacy over the battle area, destroying about 150 enemy aircraft. And the 11th Hussars continued to advance, reaching El Agheila on 8 February and ranging ahead on the road towards Sirte.

But sheer success precipitated an acute dilemma. The way seemed open for the conquest of the whole of Italian North Africa – if Greece remained unassisted. Wavell signalled Dill in London on the 10th: 'Extent of Italian defeat at Benghazi makes it seem possible that Tripoli might yield to small force if despatched without undue delay. Am working out commitment involved but hesitate to advance further in view of Balkan situation.' The Defence Committee met at Ten Downing Street at 9.30 p.m. on this Monday to discuss the question of priorities. These had been further complicated by an apparent reversal of Greek policy. Metaxas had died in the last days of January; the British Ambassador, Sir Michael Palairet, had asked the new Council leader, Koryzis, if Athens remained reluctant to receive British aid. Koryzis astonished the Ambassador by replying he had never seen statements expressing such reluctance, and next day the British were asked whether their offer of help still existed. The Defence Committee meeting on the 10th therefore agreed that: 'The Commanders-in-Chief (Middle East) had been told after the capture of Tobruk that the European situation must take priority over future African operations, although they might go for Benghazi if the going was good. It would

34

be wrong to alter this decision ... We should adhere to our existing policy of stopping when a secure flank has been gained by the capture of Benghazi.' No further advance would be made to take advantage of the Italian collapse and to secure Italian North Africa; troops should be shifted to the Balkans instead. At another meeting of the Defence Committee next day, 11 February, Ministers agreed Anthony Eden and Sir John Dill should fly out to the Middle East immediately to co-ordinate action. Wavell's orders, drafted by Churchill, were despatched early on Wednesday, 12 February:

> If Greece, with British aid, can hold up for some months German advance, chances of Turkish intervention will be favoured. Therefore it would seem that we should try to get in a position to offer ... transfer to Greece of the fighting portion of the Army which has hitherto defended Egypt and make every plan for sending and reinforcing it to the limit.

Orders were already being prepared in Cairo to whittle down and re-deploy the Middle East forces: the army in Cyrenaica would be reduced to one division and one armoured brigade, the minimum which Wavell considered feasible; divisions had to be reformed, large units had to be replaced by smaller, supply bases had to be diminished, and hundreds of administrative details attended to which were involved in the switch from North Africa to the Balkans. 'We must get tidied up,' understated Wavell.

   On this same day, 12 February, a senior German officer, to be described by a British Intelligence summary next month as 'obscure', set foot in Tripoli to command German troops sent to assist the shattered Italians – Lieutenant-General Erwin Rommel. The 'Desert Fox' had arrived.

Chapter 2

'Battleaxe'

Within minutes of his arrival in North Africa at noon on 12 February, Rommel was in close conference with Gariboldi, Italian C-in-C in Tripoli and technically his superior. Rommel urged a plan for 'not a step further back, powerful *Luftwaffe* support and every available man to be thrown in for the defence of the Sirte sector'. With his usual speed, he had decided 'in view of the tenseness of the situation and the sluggishness of the Italian command, to depart from my instructions to confine myself to a reconnaissance and to take command at the front'. Rommel, for a short while, would be a General without an army: the first German units had still to arrive. Yet during the afternoon of his day of arrival he flew over the battle-area, and immediately issued orders for Italian troop movements. Italian formations, including the *Ariete* armoured division, were hurried forward to Sirte, and the first German troops disembarking at Tripoli on the 14th were at the front within twenty-six hours; on the 17th Rommel wrote to his wife: 'Everything's splendid with me and mine in this glorious sunshine …' Next day Hitler announced in Berlin that German troops in North Africa would henceforth be known as the *Afrika Korps*.

Eden and Dill had left London on their mission to the Middle East on the same day that Rommel reached Tripoli – and the same day that Wavell received his orders to shift priority to the Balkans. The War Secretary had been given an extremely powerful brief by the Prime Minister: he would represent the British Government in all diplomatic and military matters, and above all had power to act on his own initiative in an emergency without reference to the War Cabinet in London. The party reached Cairo on the 19th, a few hours after Hitler had issued further orders in Berlin: troops crossing into Bulgaria for advance on Greece would commence on 2 March. Eden and Dill found Wavell now in full agreement that a German move upon Greece seemed imminent, and the Middle East Commander also agreed that Britain's ally should be helped; as the General had declared in an appreciation completed during the 19th: 'We have a difficult choice, but I think we are more likely to be playing the enemy's game by remaining inactive than by taking action in the Balkans. Provided that conversation with the Greeks show there is a good chance of establishing a front against the Germans with our assistance, I think we should take it.' He downgraded the chances of a German–Italian counter-attack in Cyrenaica – the enemy did not have sufficient command of the sea to pass through the considerable convoys that would be needed; moreover,

Opposite A British tank narrowly escapes the effects of a German bomb.

37

the Germans lacked any practical desert-warfare experience, and were deficient in transport. A meeting held in Cairo on the morning of the 20th therefore agreed that all possible help should be given to Greece, if, in Wavell's words, 'a good chance' existed of establishing a front against invasion.

Back in London on the same day, Churchill apparently showed hesitation at a War Cabinet meeting:

> It was possible, of course, that before making the advance the Germans would offer the Greeks such attractive terms that they would feel bound to make peace. In that case we could not very well blame them ... We should have done our duty and should have to content ourselves by making our position in the Greek Islands as strong as possible ... The question of advancing into Tripoli would again arise.

The Prime Minister also commented: 'There were signs of German infiltration into North Africa.' But a signal from Eden was already *en route*, outlining the decision taken at the Cairo meeting and adding: 'If the help we can offer is accepted by the Greeks, we believe that there is a fair chance of halting a German advance.' Eden, Dill, Wavell, Longmore – the RAF Middle East Commander – and Captain Dick, representing Admiral Cunningham, flew to Athens on the 22nd and long discussions with the Greeks finally resulted in important decisions. In view of Yugoslavia's doubtful attitude the only defensive line that could be held, giving time for troop withdrawal from Albania and North Africa, was the seventy-mile 'Aliakhmon' position, running from the sea west of the Vardar River, north-west to the Yugoslav border. This would mean sacrificing Salonica, unless Yugoslavia could be brought in – Eden undertook another attempt to persuade her. The Greeks would begin immediate preparations to withdraw to the Aliakhmon line; work would start on vital communication; British troops under General Maitland Wilson would move from Egypt as soon as possible.

As a result of optimistic signals from Eden, the War Cabinet endorsed this policy at a meeting held at 5 p.m. on the 24th, and in doing so put the final seal on the abandonment of an aggressive policy in North Africa. This Monday also saw the first small engagement between British and *Afrika Korps* units; the British suffered most.

Eden failed in his attempts to bring both Turkey and Yugoslavia in on the side of Greece; the War Cabinet decided help must still be sent, even though the Chiefs of Staff had considered on the 24th that Turkish or Yugoslav support would be essential. Then, on the last day of February, small advanced German formations crept

Another of Wavell's responsibilities: Kenya, where 75,000 troops were involved in 1940, drawing away strength from North Africa. Now Greece would be added to Wavell's burdens.

from Roumania and rumbled across the icy Danube into Bulgaria. The preliminary advance upon Greece had begun. Two days later the main elements of the German 12th Army flooded into Bulgaria, and Eden and Dill hurried back to Athens – where they found, to their appalled dismay, that the Greek attitude had changed disastrously. Withdrawal to the Aliakhmon line had not started; Greek forces risked being caught out in the open. Wavell's proviso that a 'good chance' should exist of stopping the German advance had been shattered. The British commander rushed to Athens, and attempts to sort out the mess were made during the next 'indescribably anxious' forty-eight hours. In the end Eden and his party felt obliged to accept a Greek offer of sixteen to twenty-three battalions for the Aliakhmon line, instead of the thirty-five battalions which the British had been led to expect. British troops would therefore have far less Greek support, would have inadequate preparations, and a deficient communications system. The War Cabinet, after a critical delay in signals between Eden and London lasting almost three days, could only support the decision already taken by Eden on the spot. Troops continued to move from North Africa, leaving the reduced force facing the Germans and Italians in Cyrenaica.

'Speed is the thing that matters here,' wrote Rommel to his wife on 5 March. British attention remained riveted on the Balkans. German troops continued to surge south, while militarily the Greeks were further extended and weakened in Albania after repulsing a new Italian offensive on the 8th. The British 1st Armoured Brigade landed and began to move north, but these units would not

39

German infantrymen
encircle Marsa el Brega,
waiting for the Panzers
to take possession.

reach the forward area until 27 March. British air strength in the
country only numbered eighty operational aircraft; the Germans
would be able to employ eight hundred over the battle area. In
North Africa, Rommel continued to prepare his plans. He flew to
Hitler's HQ on the 19th, and his scheme for vigorous action in the
desert received an apparent setback; according to von Brauchitsch,
Commander-in-Chief of the German Army, 'there was no intention
of striking a decisive blow in Africa in the near future'. Hitler, like
the British, remained preoccupied with Yugoslavia and Greece.
But Rommel was still convinced that the temporary British weakness in Cyrenaica 'should have been exploited with the utmost
energy' and he returned to Tripoli determined to disregard Hitler's
cautious directive. At the same time Wavell visited his forward
units, and immediately became seriously disturbed by the state of
the cruiser tanks in the 2nd Armoured Division, by the troop dispositions, and by the general handling of the situation by his army
commander, Neame. 'I came back anxious and depressed from this
visit, but there was nothing much I could do about it. The movement to Greece was in full swing and I had nothing left in the bag.
But I had forebodings and my confidence in Neame was shaken.'
Back in Cairo he issued detailed orders: he envisaged fighting and
limited withdrawal if the enemy undertook a cautious and limited
advance, during which the British should retain freedom of movement and initiative. 'Time is pressing,' he told Neame. 'You
must put all necessary moves and work in hand without delay.'

40

British Ministers met at Ten Downing Street at 5 p.m. on Monday, 24 March, to hear gloomy news of Atlantic sinkings, on the over-stretch of the Royal Navy, and on recent heavy bombing raids on Britain. A note was hurried into the Cabinet Room: 'According to a message just received from Belgrade, the Yugoslav Prime Minister and Foreign Minister were leaving that night for Vienna to sign a pact with Germany.' Greece had apparently lost all hope of vital Yugoslav support; the whole weight of the German assault would be launched against the northern Greek frontier; the position of the British troops had been rendered even more hopeless. And on the same day Rommel began his moves in the desert. Before his recent visit to Hitler's HQ he had instructed his 5th Light Division to plan a limited assault on the British outposts at El Agheila on the Tripoli border; now, on the 24th, the attack went in and British deficiencies were fully revealed. Rommel prepared for his next, far larger, operation, while Churchill despatched an anxious cable to Wavell on the 26th: 'We are naturally concerned at rapid German advance to El Agheila. It is their habit to push on whenever they are not resisted. I presume you are only waiting for the tortoise to stick his head out far enough before chopping it off ...' Never again would Rommel be described as a tortoise; instead he would soon acquire the distinction of being the only German general to be mentioned in War Cabinet discussions by name, rather than being anonymously described as 'the enemy commander'. Events also quickened to a climax in both North Africa and the Balkans. On Thursday, 27 March, a military *coup* took place in Yugoslavia, overthrowing the Government which had sought agreement with the Nazis, and at the same time the first British troops reached the Aliakhmon position in Greece. Hopes were again raised that the Germans might be repulsed, with Yugoslav help. But Hitler, thrown into one of the most violent rages of his life, ordered his military chiefs to 'destroy Yugoslavia militarily as a nation'. The attack on Yugoslavia – and on Greece – would be launched at the beginning of April.

Rommel moved first. On 30 March Wavell informed Neame of reports of large German forces landing at Tripoli, although he added: 'I do not believe that he [the enemy] can make any big effort for at least another month.' Next day, at about 9 a.m., Rommel threw his forces forward. 'It was a chance I could not resist,' he wrote. The German 3rd Reconnaissance Unit and 5th Panzer Regiment struck at advance units of the British 2nd Armoured Division between Marada and Marsa el Brega, and despite a courageous British defence, the enemy had taken the position by nightfall. Rommel sent a typically terse order: 'Push on!' German reinforcements were rushed forward to accelerate the British withdrawal, and by 2 April enemy troops had battled their way through the sand to Agedabia, which fell during the day. 'I decided to stay on the heels of the retreating enemy and make a bid to seize the whole of Cyrenaica at one stroke,' commented Rommel.

Wavell reported to the Chiefs of Staff on the 2nd: 'Losses not serious at present, but the mechanical condition of the Armoured Brigade is causing Neame much concern ... As I can produce no more armoured units for at least three or four weeks, I have warned him to keep three brigades in being, even if it involves considerable withdrawal, possibly even from Benghazi.' He decided to replace Neame, whom he believed to have lost control, then temporised by having O'Connor stay with Neame during the battle to provide support. Rommel seized upon the British command confusion and weakness on the ground, boldly separating his forces to threaten from both the coastal and desert directions, and urging his units forward at maximum speed – despite misgivings voiced by his subordinate commanders over the state of the German vehicles. 'One cannot permit unique opportunities to slip by for the sake of trifles.' By 4 April the British were in full retreat and the German 3rd Reconnaissance Unit entered Benghazi during the day, to find masses of valuable British equipment and the port virtually intact. 'Dearest Lu,' wrote Rommel to his wife. 'We've been attacking since the 31st with dazzling success ... I took the risk against all orders and instructions because the opportunity seemed favourable.'

Churchill wired an urgent signal to Eden, still in Greece. 'Evacuation Benghazi serious, will probably deny us use of Tobruk ... Far more important than the loss of ground is the idea that we cannot face the Germans and that their appearance is enough to drive us back.' Rommel had set his sights on Mechili, the main British base in Cyrenaica, and by now he had divided his advance into three deadly prongs. On the left would continue the push down the coast road; in the centre would strike armoured forces aiming at Mechili via Antelat and Msus, while the Italian *Ariete* would also push towards Mechili through a flanking movement. The British continued to fall back, and by the 5th Rommel could issue another curt command: 'Mechili clear of enemy. Make for it. Drive fast.' By 6 April the German fingers were curling around this vital area, from which the enemy could control the exit bottleneck from Cyrenaica.

42   And also on Sunday, 6 April, Hitler declared war on Yugoslavia

and Greece. Only ninety-five minutes after his hysterical announcement, mass German bomber formations clustered over the largely undefended Yugoslav capital, and for the next seventy-two hours the *Luftwaffe* battered Belgrade into mounds of smoking rubble, slaughtering seventeen thousand civilians. Other German aircraft struck at Piraeus while enemy ground formations swept over the Greek frontier. Ten German divisions would eventually be thrown against two divisions of British, Australian and New Zealand troops. Clearly no reinforcements could be sliced from the reeling British forces in North Africa, and, also late on the 6th, Wavell suffered another severe setback. Neame and O'Connor fell into German hands as they drove from Mechili, and two other British generals, Rimington and Gambier-Parry, were captured at about the same time. Wavell had to fly up to the battle-area himself, taking with him his only spare commander, General J. D. Lavarack of the 7th Australian Division. 'Position in Western Desert greatly deteriorated yesterday,' reported Wavell to London on the 7th, 'due to enemy moving on Mechili by desert route and further vehicle losses of 2nd Armoured Division by mechanical breakdown and air bombing. Third Armoured Division has little or no fighting value and losses and state of Indian motor brigade are not known.'

Two hours after this cable arrived, the War Cabinet met to discuss the acutely depressing Balkan and North African situations.

Fort Mechili, Rommel's target: the position commanded the desert track south of the Derna coastal road.

The Prime Minister re-read a signal sent by Wavell five weeks previously which had given 'a hopeful appreciation of the situation in Cyrenaica and the scale of attack likely to be expected ...' Churchill declared: 'The War Cabinet decision regarding assistance to Greece had largely been founded on this appreciation.' Clearly, Wavell could expect to receive the brunt of the blame for the gross deficiencies in British strength both in the Balkans and in Africa – over which, in fact, he had no control. Churchill told the War Cabinet that all efforts must be made to stop the German advance at Tobruk. 'Tobruk was a strongly fortified place and the German force which had advanced so rapidly could hardly possess the necessary artillery to reduce it. If we could hold the advance at Tobruk we would be well satisfied. But we must recognise that this might not be possible.' Despite Churchill's cautionary final words, he sent a stiff signal to Wavell immediately after the Ten Downing Street meeting: 'You should surely be able to hold Tobruk with its permanent Italian defences, at least until or unless the enemy brings up strong artillery forces. It seems difficult to believe that he can do this for some weeks ... Tobruk therefore seems to be a place to be held to the death.'

Wavell had already come to the same conclusion, and by the time this signal reached Cairo at 3 a.m. on the 8th, the British commander was flying to Tobruk in an unreliable Hudson; he landed amidst sand squalls to settle the details of the Tobruk defences. Wavell left in the afternoon of the 8th, after which oil pressure failure in his aircraft forced a detour to abandoned El Adem. He escaped from this outpost, likely to be overrun at any moment, only to be brought down in the desert by renewed engine failure. For about eight anxious hours his HQ at Cairo were without contact with their commanding officer, until his staff were relieved to hear early on the 9th that Wavell and his party had been found by a Sudanese patrol. On reaching Cairo the tired Wavell immediately replied to Churchill's signal concerning Tobruk, and the message revealed the continued anxiety felt by the British commander. 'Although first enemy effort seems to have exhausted itself, I do not feel we shall have long respite and am still very anxious. Tobruk is not good defensive position.' Churchill received this gloomy assessment at the same time as ominous reports reached London from Greece. The Germans had entered Salonica at 4 a.m. on the 9th, and General Wilson, whose troops had had insufficient time to settle into the weak Aliakhmon line, ordered the first British withdrawal during the day, to begin on the night of the 11th.

Rommel wrote in his diary: 'The reconquest of Cyrenaica was

now complete. However, it still seemed to me very important to remain on the enemy's heels.' He felt his advance had by no means finished; likewise, his opposing commander realised with Churchill that Tobruk must be defended to the last. Yet Wavell warned London: 'My resources are very limited, especially of mobile and armoured troops and of anti-tank and anti-aircraft weapons. It will be a race against time.' Churchill sent an immediate reply, dated 10 April: 'We all cordially endorse your decision to hold Tobruk and will do all in our power to bring you aid.' While German Stukas screamed down on the defences, troops at Tobruk worked in a frenzy to prepare for the inevitable tank attack.

German guns open the bombardment in the siege of Tobruk.

The 9th Australian Division, already tired after a tough rear-guard action at Derna, was gathered in, soon to be reinforced by the 18th Brigade from the Australian 7th Division which had previously been earmarked for Greece. Commander of these Australians would be Major-General Leslie Morshead, a man of ideal temperament to withstand the siege; he told his commanders: 'There'll be no Dunkirk here. If we should have to get out, we shall fight our way out. There is to be no surrender and no retreat.' From the start he insisted upon an aggressive defence, and when Rommel rushed his units into the first assault on Tobruk late on the 12th he found unexpectedly stubborn opposition. The defences were 45

British troops resting under the shade of roadside pepper trees during the retreat in Greece.

pounded again on Sunday, 13 April, with Rommel once more displaying his incredible energy. 'I drove up to a point about 100 yards south of the wire to see for myself how the operation was developing,' he wrote. 'We were forced to withdraw after the aerial of our signals vehicle had been cut through by a splinter ... I spurred the division to the utmost speed ... the driver of the Mammoth was wounded by a bullet which came through the visor ... I climbed into the driving seat and drove myself ...'

But by now Morshead had organised his forces into six brigades of infantry, four regiments of field artillery armed with 25-pounders, two anti-tank regiments, sixteen heavy AA and fifty-nine light AA guns, and the 3rd Armoured Brigade with twenty-six cruiser, fifteen light and four infantry tanks. These units proved sufficient to beat off the Germans on the 13th and again on the night of the 13th/14th. Another attempt to take Tobruk on the 16th/17th, this time by the Italians, met with even less success. The German commander ordered his troops to by-pass the port and continue the advance into Egypt towards Sollum, but the Australians at Tobruk would remain between this light forward force and the bulk of Rommel's army, imposing a constant threat to his communications. Wavell, in an assessment written in mid-April, allowed some cautious optimism. 'I can see no hope of being able to relieve Tobruk for at least several months. Whether the garrison can hold out long enough will remain to be seen ... But the enemy's difficulties are great.'

In Greece, the situation slid rapidly from bad to worse. British and Greek troops were being pressed back on all fronts and complete collapse seemed inevitable. British Ministers met at Ten Downing Street at 9.30 p.m. on the 16th to hear a telegram just received from Wavell.

> Have received following from Wilson timed 1700 hours today. Begins: 'Just had conversation with Papagos who described Greek army as being severely pressed and getting in administrative difficulties owing to air action ... Papagos also suggested that as things may become critical in future we should re-embark British troops and save Greece from devastation.'

Ministers agreed the Greek offer should be accepted, and British troops should sail once endorsement of Papagos' suggestion had been obtained from the Greek Government. Yugoslavia capitulated on the 17th, releasing more German forces for the Greek offensive. General 'Jumbo' Wilson drove to the Greek Palace to meet the King and the Greek leaders agreed to a British withdrawal; Koryzis, the Prime Minister, said his Government stood ready to prejudice the safety of Greek troops to aid the British, since they regarded themselves as hosts. Within twenty-four hours Koryzis had committed suicide.

Organised Greek resistance ended on 24 April, and on the night of this Thursday the British evacuation, 'Demon', began, to continue for almost a week. Only 15,361 of the troops were taken direct to Egypt, with the rest going to Crete. About twelve thousand men were left behind, dead or missing, plus much valuable equipment. And Crete became the next German target. Wavell, exhausted already from the tense North African campaign, from troubles in Iraq and from a possible German threat to Egypt from Syria, now had to supervise the defence of the island, which would be commanded by the brave New Zealander, Major-General Bernard Freyberg, VC.

Moreover, Rommel might be expected to renew his offensive at any moment, despite the over-extension of his forces. The British army in the desert suffered drastically from equipment shortages, especially tanks; Wavell cabled Dill on the 18th: 'Consider provision of cruiser repeat cruiser tanks vital addition to infantry tanks which lack speed and radius of action for desert operations. CIGS please give your personal assistance.' Churchill reacted immediately, obtaining reluctant Chiefs of Staff approval for the despatch of tanks direct through the Mediterranean. Over three hundred of Britain's best tanks left on their hazardous journey in the 'Tiger' convoy on the 26th. But Churchill expected a price to be paid for

Field-Marshal von
Paulus.

his help, signalling Wavell on the 22nd: 'You should furnish us with all your plans for bringing these vehicles into action at the very earliest ... no German should remain in Cyrenaica by the end of the month of June.'

Rommel was also finding himself under pressure from his superiors, although of an entirely different kind. His actions had failed to find full approval in Berlin, especially from General Franz Halder, the German Chief of Staff, who jotted in his diary: 'Reports from officers coming from this theatre as well as a personal letter show that Rommel is in no way equal to his task. He rushes about

the whole day between the widely scattered units, stages reconnaissance raids and fritters away his forces.' Halder sent General
Friedrich von Paulus to report on the desert commander – 'perhaps
the only man with sufficient personal influence to head off this
soldier gone stark mad'. Paulus, later to surrender his army to the
Russians at Stalingrad, reached North Africa at the end of April
and declared Rommel to be weak in men and material, and as not
enough could be sent across the hostile Mediterranean to fill his
requirements, Paulus therefore saw no point in sending further reinforcements to the *Afrika Korps*. This message was intercepted by
the British, and provided Churchill with further information to
prod Wavell into greater activity. Wavell sent an irritable cable to
the Prime Minister on 5 May: 'I have already issued orders for
offensive action in Western Desert at earliest possible date to be
prepared on assumption "Tiger" successful.'

British shells burst near
Halfaya Pass in a vain
attempt to prevent
German tanks from
forcing through.

The convoy arrived at Alexandria on 12 May with the loss of only
one ship, and Churchill believed Wavell now had all the tools he
needed to batter back the over-stretched *Afrika Korps*. And even
before the 'Tiger Cubs' – tanks brought on the convoy – could be
prepared for action, Wavell switched to the offensive by launching
an attack under Gott to drive the enemy from Sollum and Capuzzo.
The operation, 'Brevity', began on the 15th with two weak tank
regiments, plus the 22nd Guards Brigade, advancing to take Halfaya

49

German armour
regroups in the region
of Sidi Omar.

Pass and Capuzzo; simultaneously, British armour swept wide through Sidi Omar and reached Hafid Ridge west of Capuzzo. A counter-attack drove the Guards from Capuzzo, and Rommel retook Halfaya on the 26th. 'Brevity' had been a failure. 'Enemy proved rather stronger than we thought,' reported Wavell, 'and has forced us back on defensive till "Tiger Cubs" come into action.'

The British commander remained besieged by multiple problems in Egypt, Iraq, Syria, Abyssinia – and, on 20 May, scores of German gliders came hissing down upon the island of Crete backed by intense bomber raids. Battle raged for the next week with mounting British troop losses and with a soaring number of vital British warships and naval transports sunk in the attempt to support Freyberg's men. Evacuation started on the night of the 28th and continued until 1 June, by which time about eighteen thousand men had been rescued out of the thirty-two thousand on the island: about eighteen hundred troops and an equal number of sailors were killed. Britain seemed further than ever from seizing the Mediterranean initiative.

All hopes once more rested upon the army in the Western Desert. Back on 1 May Wavell had issued orders for preparations for the offensive in early June, code-named 'Battleaxe', and plans intensi-

Admiral Sir Andrew
Cunningham,
Commander-in-Chief of
the Mediterranean.

fied even while the battle for Crete was at its height. Wavell spent
long hours with his fellow commanders, Admiral Sir Andrew Cunningham for the Royal Navy, and Air Marshal A. W. Tedder, who
had replaced Longmore on the 18th. Pressure from London increased: the battle must begin as soon as possible. The Chiefs of
Staff told Wavell on the 28th: 'Our first object must be to gain a
decisive military success in the western desert and to destroy the
enemy armoured forces.' Churchill insisted upon adding a private
message, considered by the CIGS to be unwise, in which he reminded the British commander that with the Tiger Cubs he enjoyed definite numerical superiority. Wavell replied late the same
day: the forward move could not begin until 7 June at the earliest,
and he added: 'I think it right to inform you that the measure of
success which will attend this operation is in my opinion doubtful.'
British armoured cars were too lightly protected, infantry tanks too
slow and vulnerable, cruiser tanks had little advantage over the
medium German tanks, and technical breakdowns were still too
frequent. Wavell told Churchill: 'We shall not be able to accept
battle with perfect confidence in spite of numerical superiority.'
The Prime Minister's irritation increased, and with it his desire to
have Wavell replaced. Two days later the British general sent
another annoying telegram, in which he listed the defects found in
the Tiger Cubs; within twenty-four hours a further cable from
Cairo declared that 'Battleaxe' could not possibly be launched 51

before the 15th. Wavell's commitments remained colossal, despite the completion of the Crete evacuation on 1 June: plans were entering their final stages for a move into Syria. Wavell sent his 'Battle-axe' appreciation to London on the 6th: he intended to attempt a three-stage offensive, first an advance on enemy forces in the Sollum–Capuzzo area, second an advance to the Tobruk area and raids by the Tobruk garrison, and third, exploitation. But he warned

that reduced strength at the end of the first stage might rule out the
second and third.

Rommel fully expected the attack. Defences at Halfaya had already been strengthened, especially with an important development
introduced by the German commander: the 88-mm anti-aircraft
guns were deployed in dug-in positions to act as most effective anti-
tank weapons. Rommel believed the British had about three   53

Rommel's 'secret' weapon: he ordered 88-mm anti-aircraft guns to be well dug in and used as anti-tank guns – with deadly success.

hundred tanks for the offensive, whereas the actual number totalled about two hundred; Wavell also believed the Germans had about three hundred, whereas the total actually fell below two hundred. But Rommel had deployed his armour well, concentrating on blocking any drive along the coast towards the Sollum–Capuzzo front, and with the reserve – the 5th Light – poised ready to move forward to his right flank. Above all, his excellent wireless interception system enabled Rommel to have clear indications of British intentions.

Early on Sunday, 14 June, a signal left Cairo for General Beresford-Peirse, now commanding the troops in the desert. '"Battleaxe" is the most important operation yet undertaken in Middle East,' declared Wavell. 'Success will bring incalculable results. First decisive defeat of German troops on land will be an outstanding event … Am confident you will gain decisive victory and send you and your troops my very best wishes.' So, hiding his doubts over 'Battleaxe', Wavell then left his office to play a round of golf with Blamey, his Australian deputy: the non-military activity might help security, and besides he could do no more. While the British general still trudged around the sandy course, the first British units were beginning to move forward over the desert. Reports of the advance rapidly reached Rommel; at 9 p.m. he alerted his reserve and within hours these tanks of the 5th Light Division were creeping up to cover the right of the 15th Panzer units on the Capuzzo–Sollum front.

The main British assault began in the early hours of the 15th. The Guards Brigade managed to take Capuzzo, but elsewhere the reports from the front proved exceedingly depressing: Indian units in the northern coastal area were brought to a halt; in the centre eleven out of twelve Matildas were destroyed by the eighty-eights embedded at Halfaya and further casualties were suffered by following tanks, and in the south only forty-eight tanks from the 7th Armoured were operative at the end of the grim day's battle. The conflict was conforming to a pattern dictated by Rommel: first he intended to allow the British to wear themselves down against his defences, then, in his words: 'I planned to concentrate both armoured divisions suddenly into one focus and thus deal the enemy an unexpected blow in his most sensitive spot.' The first stage had been successfully accomplished by nightfall on the 15th, and very early on the 16th Rommel spared a moment to scribble a line to his wife. 'Today – it's 2.30 a.m. – will see the decision. It's going to be a hard fight, so you'll understand that I can't sleep.'

During the 16th tanks of the British 7th Armoured and the German 5th Light clashed near Sidi Omar; the weakened British units were unable to prevent the enemy breaking through and the Germans darted towards Sidi Suleiman. Seen from Cairo, the fight apparently hung in the balance, with Wavell reporting to London at noon on the 16th: 'General impression heavy fighting and close-run battle.' In London, War Cabinet Ministers were informed at 5 p.m. that the enemy were surrounded at Halfaya, although they were continuing to resist. 'There is no reason to be dissatisfied with the progress made, although we have had a number of tanks put out of action by mines.' But Rommel realised that the minor break-through by tanks of the 5th Light towards Sidi Suleiman could give him the opportunity he sought. He immediately forged the second arm of a pincer movement, ordering 15th Panzer to disengage, strike north, and aim for Sidi Suleiman, despite the consequent risk of leaving the area north of Capuzzo largely undefended. 'This was the turning point of the battle,' wrote Rommel.

His tanks advanced during the night of the 16th and throughout the hours of darkness the rumble of gunfire crept closer to Sidi Suleiman; by dawn the two German thrusts had started to converge. Confusion increased among the British as the threat to their communications grew. Early on the 17th the Germans intercepted a request from the commander of the 7th Armoured Division, 55

Creagh, for Beresford-Peirse to come forward: Creagh explained that he now only had twenty-two cruisers and seventeen infantry tanks left, adding that Rommel was in an excellent position to cut off all the British forces remaining at Capuzzo and Halfaya, and an 'important decision' would therefore have to be taken. Rommel commented on this intercepted message: 'It sounded suspiciously as though the British commander no longer felt himself capable of handling the situation.' Now, believed Rommel, was the time to exert maximum pressure: he ordered his pincer moves to drive for Halfaya, thus closing the net tight around Capuzzo and the bulk of the British forces.

Wavell, who had just flown up from Cairo, had been standing with Beresford-Peirse when the message came through from Creagh, and he immediately went with the desert army commander to the 7th Armoured HQ. But by the time he arrived the British had begun to withdraw. General Sir Frank Messervy, commander of the 4th Indian Division situated near Halfaya, had believed only instant retirement could save his forces, and he had given the necessary order after consultation with Creagh. The movement had already started; Wavell, even if he had wanted, could not have reversed the procedure at that stage. He therefore gave the general order for formations to break off the fight and to withdraw, collecting as many crippled tanks as possible. In the early afternoon he returned to Cairo. Armoured cars, Churchill's precious Tiger Cubs, and other valuable material now littered the scarred desert. In England, the Prime Minister had sought solitude while reports of 'Battleaxe' reached London, and he had slipped away to his Chequers home. There he received a short sad signal from Wavell. 'I regret to report failure of "Battleaxe".' Churchill shuffled out into the garden; he wrote later: 'I wandered about the valley disconsolately.'

'Dearest Lu,' wrote Rommel to his wife on the 18th. 'The three-day battle has ended in complete victory ... The joy of the "Afrika" troops over this latest victory is tremendous.' Yet Rommel, the superb realist, knew his success could only be limited: his supply lines were already fully extended, and he could not exploit the British setback; moreover, the Australians still stood firm at Tobruk. Nevertheless, the failure of 'Battleaxe' meant the end of Wavell as Middle East Commander. He took upon himself full responsibility for the setback, despite his reluctance to initiate the battle and his warnings prior to the offensive; Churchill had long since been dissatisfied with him, and now prepared a replacement. Meanwhile both sides counted the cost: the British had lost 122 men killed, 588 wounded and 259 missing, plus four guns, twenty-seven cruiser and sixty-four infantry tanks rendered inoperative through enemy action or mechanical breakdown. Aircraft losses totalled thirty-six, three of them bombers. About ninety-three German officers and men had been killed, 350 wounded and 235 missing; probably about fifty tanks had broken down during the battle, and the British had destroyed a further dozen. Ten German aircraft had been brought down.

In the early evening of 20 June Churchill sent over to the War Office copies of two signals he wanted despatched: one would go to the Viceroy of India to be handed to General Sir Claude Auchinleck, C-in-C India, and the other would be transmitted to Wavell in Cairo.

I have come to the conclusion [declared the latter signal] that public interest will best be served by appointment of General Auchinleck to relieve you ... I have greatly admired your command and conduct of these armies both in success and adversity ... I feel however that after the long strain you have borne, a new eye and a new hand are required in this most seriously menaced theatre.

The Prime Minister added: 'You should proceed at your earliest convenience to India.' The signal reached Cairo forty-eight hours later, and Wavell sent a dignified reply on the same day: 'I think you are wise to make change and get new ideas and action on the many problems in the Middle East and am sure Auchinleck will be successful choice.' A request by Wavell for a brief home leave was refused by the Prime Minister, with Churchill reported to have declared: 'I can't have him hanging about in London living in his club.' Other more probable reasons were the need for speed and the need to avoid an unsettled vacuum in either Egypt or India. On 30 June the austere, distinguished General Sir Claude Auchinleck arrived at the Cairo HQ; five days later Wavell departed, leaving a remarkable achievement: British control had been extended from Kenya to the Turkish frontier through often simultaneous operations in Abyssinia, Kenya, Syria, Iraq, the Western Desert. Despite the failure of 'Battleaxe', his previous victories in North Africa would mean that the Italian Army would never be the same again. Strains had been colossal for Wavell, even apart from the campaigns in Greece and Crete. His legacy remained awesome; now the 'Auk', outwardly self-confident but secretly shy and sensitive, had been handed the burden.

Chapter 3

'Crusader'

An attempt had been made to smooth Auchinleck's path by General Sir John Dill, the CIGS. A 'personal and secret' letter for the new Middle East Commander had left London on 26 June, in which Dill had admitted that Wavell had been pressed into attacking in the Western Desert before being fully prepared. 'The fault was not Wavell's except in so far as he did not resist the pressure from Whitehall with sufficient vigour.' Auchinleck might suffer similar treatment. '*You* should make it quite clear what risks are involved if a course of action is forced upon you which, from the military point of view, is undesirable. You may even find it necessary, in the extreme case, to dissociate yourself from the consequences.' Dill promised his backing. Auchinleck would also receive help from administrative changes introduced in early June. On 5 July Oliver Lyttelton, previously President of the Board of Trade, arrived in Cairo as a Minister of State to act as the War Cabinet's representative on the spot: his duties were to relieve the service commanders of 'extraneous responsibilities', to provide political guidance, and to settle matters between local authorities, for example with the Free French. Lyttelton would preside over a Middle East Defence Committee. The experiment proved successful, reducing the interference in theatre affairs by the War Cabinet in London: Lyttelton and Auchinleck struck up a firm relationship, with the former soon made well aware of the difficulties which the commander had to face. Nevertheless, these difficulties remained large; nor did pressure from Churchill diminish.

Even before Auchinleck's official take-over on 5 July the Prime Minister had begun to harry the new commander into vigorous action: a signal on 1 July urged an offensive in the Western Desert as early as possible. Auchinleck soon proved stubborn: he replied on the 4th that Syria must first be settled, and that forces required for a determined desert offensive would total two and probably three armoured divisions, plus a motorised division. By now the Germans had invaded Russia, and while the Soviets were holding on at the moment, few expected this to last; Churchill related the two theatres in his next signal to Auchinleck, dated 6 July. 'Our Intelligence shows considerable Italian reinforcements in Libya, but little or no German. However, a Russian collapse might soon alter this.' He pointed out that Auchinleck would have 500 tanks by the end of July. 'It is difficult to see how your situation is going to be better after the middle of September than it is now, and it may well worsen.'

Auchinleck remained unmoved. His reply on the 15th acknow-

Opposite General Auchinleck takes over the command of the Middle East Forces.

Temporary stalemate: a barrier across the road marks the front line.

ledged that British strength would indeed total 500 tanks, but no more than 350 could be expected to be operational after allowance for reserves and repairs. He expressed fears of a German advance from the north, through Turkey, hence rendering an early British offensive westwards in the desert even more unwise. Churchill's disappointment, already rising rapidly, soared with Auchinleck's apparently lukewarm attitude towards prized Tobruk: 'I cannot be confident that Tobruk can be maintained after September.' The Defence Committee, meeting on 17 July, agreed with Churchill's suggestion that 150 of the latest cruiser tanks should be sent out as soon as possible, if Auchinleck would agree to a strong offensive by the end of September. Auchinleck remained adamant, in a reply to London on the 23rd. 'I must repeat that to launch an offensive with the inadequate means at present at our disposal is not in my opinion a justifiable operation.'

Deadlock had apparently been reached; Churchill summoned Auchinleck home for urgent talks, and the commander arrived on the 29th to give his situation report to the War Cabinet on the 31st. In Libya, he declared, 'we had not enough armoured forces to attack. While the enemy was better off in this respect, it did not appear that he intended to make an early attack. His supply situation was precarious, thanks to the attacks on his bases and communications by the Royal Navy and RAF.' Tobruk was safe for the moment, added the general, but he reported that an offensive would be premature. Churchill declared his opposition at a Defence Committee discussion next day.

Very great efforts had been made and were being made to pour troops and equipment into the Middle East, and yet we were now told that nothing could be done until 1 November ... It would be a very great reflection on us, if in this vital period when the Russians were bearing the full brunt of the attack, and when conditions were so favourable, we took no action of any kind.

Auchinleck retorted that 'the necessity for action was obvious but the means were not so easy'. All experience showed, he continued, that a major offensive could hardly succeed in the desert without about a two to one superiority, which Britain would not have before 1 November. And so the argument continued throughout the day. Auchinleck refused to alter his opinion. Churchill wrote later:

He certainly shook my military advisers with all the detailed arguments he produced. I was myself unconvinced. But General Auchinleck's unquestioned abilities, his powers of exposition, his high, dignified and commanding personality, gave me the feeling that he might after all be right, and that even if wrong he was still the best man.

Auchinleck's date of 1 November therefore remained the target for launching the offensive.

Rommel also had problems with his superiors. The *Afrika Korps* needed maximum reinforcements and these failed to arrive, for two reasons: first, colossal forces were being sent to the Russian front, and second, the Royal Navy and RAF continued to strike against Rommel's fragile supply lines across the Mediterranean. Between July and November almost fifty Axis ships were sunk, carrying a total of 200,000 tons of supplies. General Fritz Bayerlein, the *Afrika Korps'* Chief of Staff, wrote: 'By the end of September, only a third of the troops and a seventh of the supplies which we needed had arrived. This was a terrible handicap in our race for time with the British.' Moreover, Rommel had still to contend with Tobruk, where the garrison continued to display resilience despite attempts by the Australian Government to have troops relieved – causing an additional upset for Auchinleck. Tobruk remained Rommel's prime target, and the desire to take this port became almost an obsession. Four Italian divisions and three German battalions were tied down in the seige, and, because this concentration brought with it the danger of a British strike against the German rear, Rommel had to deploy the bulk of his mobile forces between Capuzzo and Bir el Gubi.

Both commanders therefore struggled to build up their forces: Auchinleck for a full-scale advance, and Rommel for his assault on Tobruk. On 14 September the German commander launched a limited frontier offensive, aimed at probing the British positions to find out Auchinleck's intentions. The raid, 'Midsummer Night's Dream', lulled Rommel into a false sense of security: he believed the

British were not yet ready to act and that he himself therefore had more time. On 26 October he issued orders that the German offensive would not be launched until at least 15 November. Auchinleck had indeed found that his provisional date of 1 November for the offensive had been over-optimistic: Churchill and his colleagues were appalled to hear on 17 October that the opening of the attack would be postponed, due to the late arrival of reinforcements and the need to modify tanks before they could be considered suitable for desert warfare. But the revised British date was to be sooner than Rommel anticipated: Auchinleck now declared that the British attack, 'Crusader', would begin on the 15th. Both the Germans and the British were therefore aiming at approximately the same date. Tension rose daily in the respective headquarters.

> I am not nervous about 'Crusader', [confided Auchinleck in a private letter to General Hastings Ismay, Churchill's representative on the COS] but I wonder if you and those others who sit at the council table with you realise ... how everything hangs on the tactical issue of one day's fighting, and on one man's tactical ability on that one day ... Rather a terrifying thought?

With the equipment for both sides came the new manpower drafts: Germans, British, Italians, Australians, New Zealanders, South Africans ... all poured into the respective base camps to be subjected to strange routines in the unfamiliar climate.

> Each morning, [wrote Private Crimp in his diary] we rise to the strains of Rouse as first light is stealing over the desert, and after washing and shaving (in cold water) at the ablution benches, do half an hour's PT on a patch of flinty sand adjacent to the tent line ... After breakfast, training commences at 0800 hrs. – maybe a route-march, platoon exercises, lectures or desert-driving till mid-day. Some people have been put on a 'hardening-course', and spend hours in the heat indulging in jog-trots over the desert ...

Training intensified during September and October, and those fresh men at the base camps now found themselves moving forward towards the distant desert front. 'My number's come up ... It's curious how discomforting the sudden crystallisation of the future can be.' Troops flowed to the British front on the 'Western Desert Special' – a slow tedious train journey across mile after mile of pale sand. 'In some areas sandstorms are blowing and the desert is obscured in pallid, sunlit wooliness. We close the wooden compartment shutters, but the driving dust seeps through, and the atmosphere inside is like a fog.' It took time to grow accustomed to the scenery and life in the forward areas: acre upon acre of almost featureless wilderness.

> The desert, omnipresent, so saturates consciousness that it makes the mind as sterile as itself. It's only now you realise how much you normally live through the senses. Here there's nothing for them. Nothing in the landscape to rest or distract the eye; nothing to hear, but roaring truck-engines; and nothing to smell but carbon exhaust fumes and the reek of petrol. Even food tastes insipid, because of the heat, which stultifies appetite.

Men learnt to live with minimum requirements, and ordinary items normally taken for granted became precious commodities – soap, razor-blades, cleaning rags, articles of clothing – men learnt to scrounge and to steal. But they also became hardened to the climate and fit for the coming fight, and the Western Desert Force now received the title which it would carry proudly to fame – the 8th Army.

For both sides, the days of early November passed with frightening speed. So much remained to be done: tanks to be modified and tested, ammunition and fuel to be stockpiled. The target date, 15 November, came and went without the start of 'Crusader'. Auchinleck had needed a further delay, but this time only amounting to hours. On Sunday, 16 November, one junior British officer, Captain Sean Fielding, scribbled in his stained diary: 'There is battle in the air; I swear there is. It lies thick on the palate.' Rumours increased among the men during the day and troops made ready. 'Hours of checking and re-checking stores and kit and going over the MT against a sudden order to move. Maps, talcs, compass, glasses, arms and ammunition, food … and, most important, water.' An infantry private experienced this same stomach-tightening anticipation. 'It's obvious a push will be on very shortly indeed. The usual inertia of desert life has given way to a rarefied nervous alacrity. All kinds of inspections have been held – weapons, reserve rations, petrol, etc …' New ammunition had been issued and men sat in the sand sorting these piles into tracer, armour-piercing and ordinary rounds, then fitting them into clips and bandoliers while platoon-sergeants took names and addresses of next-of-kin and checked identity discs. At 9 p.m. on the 16th the rumours were confirmed when General Sir Alan Cunningham, now commander of the 8th Army, gave a briefing to senior officers. 'I am going to seek old Rommel out and destroy him and his armour.'

The basic 'Crusader' plan worked out by Auchinleck and Cunningham involved drawing forward and engaging the Panzers in a situation most favourable to the British. A new formation had been created for this purpose, the 30th Corps, comprising the 7th Armoured Division, the 1st South African Division and the 22nd Guards Brigade. This primarily armoured and mobile

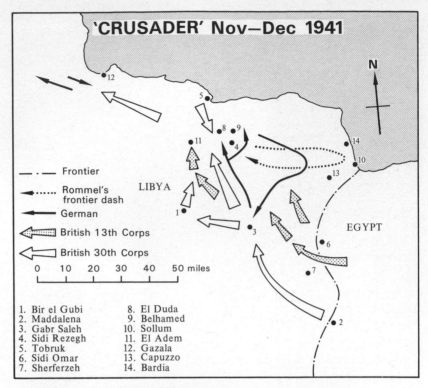

'CRUSADER' Nov—Dec 1941

N

LIBYA

EGYPT

—— · —— Frontier

◀----- Rommel's
frontier dash

◀—— German

◁▨▨▨ British 13th Corps

◁—— British 30th Corps

0   10   20   30   40   50 miles

1. Bir el Gubi   8. El Duda
2. Maddalena   9. Belhamed
3. Gabr Saleh   10. Sollum
4. Sidi Rezegh   11. El Adem
5. Tobruk   12. Gazala
6. Sidi Omar   13. Capuzzo
7. Sherferzeh   14. Bardia

formation would swing across the frontier near Fort Maddalena and
northwards to Gabr Saleh, towards the important Sidi Rezegh
escarpment, drawing Rommel's armour onwards to destruction.
Only then, after defeating the enemy tanks, would the Tobruk
garrison attempt to break out and link with the advancing British.
On the right the second of the 8th Army's two corps, the 13th, would
move south of Sidi Omar to contain and envelop the frontier
defences. The 13th Corps was basically composed of infantry units –
the 4th Indian Division and the New Zealand Division, with two
tank brigades. According to the official history, the British began
with a numerical superiority in front-line tanks: 477 excluding
those with the 13th Corps, compared to Rommel's 390. Moreover,
Cunningham had about 250 tanks behind the front-line in depots
and workshops, with over 200 on their way from England, whereas
Rommel had virtually no reserve strength. The RAF had about 550
aircraft operational at the start of the battle, compared to the
Luftwaffe total of 342.

British armour and infantry columns moved to their assembly
points during the night of the 16th and throughout the 17th. Stocks
of fuel and water were still being carried forward: supply transports
alone consumed about 180,000 gallons a day, and water would

A Bofors gun being rushed forward, passing a dead German.

remain short despite the laying of 160 miles of pipe and the building of seven pumping stations and nine reservoirs during the previous weeks. Cunningham checked his final deployment; Rommel, attending talks in Rome, returned to the desert on the night of the 17th. Also, late on the 17th, the British attempted a daring move to assassinate the 'Desert Fox': a commando group under Colonel Keyes slipped ashore from a submarine near Apollonia to attack the house where it was believed Rommel lived. But the house was now only used by his Quartermaster's staff; Keyes died in the operation, to be awarded a posthumous VC.

Only hours remained before the strike by the 30th Corps into Libya. Dark clouds suddenly split and lightning flashed vivid above the glistening waiting tanks; thunder rumbled and crashed like gunfire, and cold rain sluiced upon the hot desert sand. Commands crackled over the tank radio networks and the monstrous black hulks began to creak forward for the most violent battle of the desert war. 'There is a prayer to be said for the success of our cause,' wrote Captain Fielding, 'and I shall say it kneeling in the sand.' British tank radios were now silent as the armour shuffled forward over the sodden tracks. The rain grounded the *Luftwaffe*; the British achieved complete surprise, and by 9 a.m. on the 18th the 30th Corps armour was feeding from refuelling points secretly established beyond the frontier into Libya. Onwards surged the British front, 'as though released in some gigantic race,' wrote Private Crimp in his diary. 'As far as the eye can see over the desert-face are dust-reeking lines of vehicles – pennanted tanks and armoured cars, guns and limbers, carriers, trucks and lorries – all speeding along in parallel course westwards to Libya . . .'

Throughout the day the advance continued into enemy-held

65

Shells explode near a British Brigade HQ: troops are rising after taking cover.

territory, yet the British push only brought minimum German reaction: Rommel, his eyes still turned towards Tobruk, first dismissed the British offensive as a reconnaissance force. He continued his own plans for an assault on the Tobruk garrison, whilst the leading 30th Corps units began to threaten Gabr Saleh and while the German commanders in the forward area began to show increasing apprehension. Ravenstein, commander of the 21st Panzer, sought permission from General Ludwig Crüwell, *Afrika Korps* commander, for a concentration of armoured groups for the defence of Gabr Saleh; Crüwell, himself anxious, referred the request to Rommel, who refused to give his consent, saying 'we must not lose our nerve'. But by late evening of the 18th, units of the 7th Armoured Brigade had reached Gabr Saleh; further south and on the left flank of the 30th Corps moved the 22nd Armoured Brigade and the 1st South African Division; on the right flank, 4th Armoured Brigade advanced twelve miles east of Gabr Saleh. No opposition had been encountered other than German reconnaissance armoured cars. The 13th Corps had also moved as planned and by now the 4th Indian Division lay across the frontier wire at Sherferzen, while the New Zealand Division had entered Libya a few miles to the south-west. The 'Crusader' programme seemed to be achieving startling success.

Yet Rommel's very mistakes worked to his advantage. The primary British aim, to draw out the enemy armour and lure it to destruction, was not being accomplished: Rommel's lack of reaction led to a failure to concentrate his armour, and without such concentration the British task could not be fulfilled. General Cunningham became increasingly desperate, and now made a serious mistake. Early on the 19th he began to split his forces in an attempt to seek out the enemy, even though the compact cohesion of the 30th Corps had been its greatest strength. During the 19th the 7th Armoured Brigade reached Sidi Rezegh, the 4th Armoured Brigade moved east of Gabr Saleh, and the 22nd Armoured was sent to engage the Italian *Ariete* near Bir el Gubi, where the experienced defenders repulsed the first attacks. Cunningham further dispersed his forces later in the day, sending the 7th Support Group to join the 7th Armoured Brigade at Sidi Rezegh and moving the 1st South Africans towards Bir el Gubi, while the 4th Armoured were ordered to continue to hold back at Gabr Saleh as a link with the British left flank. The Germans, on the other hand, were beginning to respond to the threat. At noon on the 19th Crüwell had again contacted Rommel with von Ravenstein's request to hurry tanks to Gabr Saleh, and this time Rommel agreed. By dusk this force of about 120 tanks was engaging the British 4th Armoured.

So the gigantic manoeuvring continued with tanks sweeping and wheeling across the desert. Units moved and clashed with the enemy in apparent uncoordinated fashion. The 22nd Armoured Division pushed against the *Ariete* Division near Bir el Gubi and destroyed thirty-five enemy tanks, but then lost fifty-five tanks, many of them breakdowns, as they tried to storm more prepared defensive positions; British units pulled back again. 'Round and about are many Italian tanks and some of ours,' wrote Captain Fielding. 'All very badly shot up and some with their dead still in them. The oddest details remain in one's mind. The commander of one Wop tank, lying dead beside his machine, had his fingers crossed; and he had absurdly small feet cased in new boots . . .' The main British and German formations failed to find one another during the 20th; 21st Panzer became stranded near Sidi Omar out of fuel, and urgent requests were made for petrol to be flown in, while the British tried to concentrate their hold on Sidi Rezegh. Now came another departure from the original 'Crusader' plan: German armour seemed to be committed elsewhere, and General W. H. E. Gott, commander of the 7th Armoured Division, believed the time had come for the Tobruk break-out, earlier than previously intended. Cunningham hesitated, then agreed this should begin the following morning, 21 November.

But the German armour remained virtually intact, and Crüwell now swung the *Afrika Korps* towards Gabr Saleh to clash with the 4th Armoured Brigade. This action, although inconclusive, led to a

67

German Pioneers taken
prisoner during confused
operations around
Tobruk: the captives
have been blindfolded
to prevent them noting
details of the British
positions.

further British mistake: field commanders reported that twenty-six
enemy tanks had possibly been destroyed, and Cunningham believed
the decisive action envisaged in the original plan was successfully
taking place. The way seemed open for the link-up with the
Tobruk garrison, if the position at Sidi Rezegh – between Gabr
Saleh and the port – could be secured. The 7th Support Group was
therefore ordered to assist the Tobruk break-out by securing the
Sidi Rezegh ridge early on the 21st, and the 5th South African
Brigade was directed to give support. The airfield at Sidi Rezegh
had already been occupied by tanks of the 7th Armoured Brigade
on the afternoon of the 19th.

Yet Rommel had by now realised the full threat confronting him
and had correctly assessed the British intentions. The Tobruk
garrison must be prevented from striking out, and the advancing
British must be blocked from taking Sidi Rezegh. During the
evening of the 20th Rommel told Crüwell to break off at Gabr
Saleh: the *Afrika Korps* must 'attack and destroy the enemy force
which has advanced on Tobruk', and at 4 a.m. on the 21st Crüwell

received a further order 'to get going in good time' as 'the situation in this whole theatre is very critical'. Rommel would direct operations to prevent the Tobruk break-out while the main *Afrika Korps* formations would battle with the British at vital Sidi Rezegh. The stage had been set for a tank battle of unprecedented ferocity – and complexity.

British troops move forward into the 'fog of war', protected by a wave of tanks and by the dust and smoke billowing across the desert.

Contrary to Cunningham's plan, Crüwell managed to disengage at Gabr Saleh, mainly through the superb *Afrika Korps* drill, and he hurried north-west towards Sidi Rezegh. There, the British had launched their main offensive against the vital northern ridge, only about twelve miles from the nearest Tobruk defences and about four miles from El Duda, the immediate objective of the garrison break-through. Brigadier J. Campbell, commander of the 7th Support Group, advanced with the 6th Royal Tanks at 8.30 a.m. on the 21st and successfully took a section of open escarpment, but the Royal Tanks met fierce opposition in attempting to push further north to El Duda. And now Crüwell's *Afrika Korps* streaked in from the south-east to launch a vigorous counter-attack. Brigadier Davy,

69

German Junkers 87 dive-bombers on their way to attack British tanks on 23 November.

commander of the 7th Armoured Brigade, left the remnants of the Royal Tanks with Campbell and moved the two other regiments in his brigade to meet this new threat. By 10 a.m. most of one of these regiments, the 7th Hussars, had been destroyed, with only twelve tanks surviving and with ammunition almost exhausted. Terrible fighting continued throughout the day, with Crüwell urging forward his panzers and with the British 4th and 22nd Armoured Brigades attempting to reinforce the battered 7th Armoured Brigade – which had now lost the 7th Hussars, most of the 2nd Rifles and many of Davy's third regiment, the 2nd Royal Tanks. Brigadier Campbell won the VC, standing in his open staff car at the front of his tanks to drive them across the sand-billowing battle-field; the British managed to hold their ground.

The 'fog of war' had rarely been so thick. German and British units were layered upon one another in a shifting, writhing mass –

70

starting from the north these layers consisted of the 70th Division, attempting to force a way from Tobruk, then German and Italian regiments facing north to seal this escape, followed by Germans and Italians facing south to oppose the remains of 7th Support Group near El Duda, then the 7th Armoured Brigade to the south-east facing Crüwell's *Afrika Korps* counter-attack, and finally the 4th and 22nd Armoured Brigades which had followed the *Afrika Korps* from Gabr Saleh. 'A complicated situation indeed,' commented the official historian, 'which, if suggested for the setting of a training exercise, must have been rejected for the reason that in real life these things simply could not happen.'

Rommel made a potentially serious mistake. By the evening of the 21st he had successfully stopped the Tobruk break-out, but he remained anxious to prevent a link between the garrison and advancing British armour at El Duda. He therefore ordered Crüwell to send tanks further north to help block this move. Crüwell hesitated, but eventually despatched the 21st Panzer to Belhamed, about four miles east of El Duda; at the same time he felt it necessary to withdraw 15th Panzer for re-grouping. The two *Afrika Korps* divisions were thus dangerously divided by about eighteen miles. On the other hand the British command were over-optimistic, believing the German moves might indicate a withdrawal. Unjustified elation clouded the true appreciation of events in the 8th Army HQ, in Cairo, and in turn in London. Confident reports reaching Whitehall, coupled with the early rapid advance into Libya, plus eye-witness descriptions such as the following, all seemed to herald a massive British victory:

> Libya is full of our troops. It is grand. Everywhere there are eager faces; convoy commanders sitting up aloft their trucks like sunburned gods – their sun compasses pointing a black sliver of shadow towards the Boche; despatch riders bumping incredibly through the sandy, rutted tracks; officers in groups, their maps on knees, listening to their orders; lorried infantry waiting, waiting, waiting; guns, their dust covers off, marching through the infantry and off to a flank with majestic indifference …

Churchill, at Ten Downing Street, prepared to make a victory speech. 'Thank you for the very full information now flowing,' he cabled Auchinleck on the 22nd. 'I might perhaps broadcast Sunday night if it seems expedient.' Later on this Saturday, 22 November, Auchinleck sent a further report to London: 'Prospects of achieving our immediate object, namely, the destruction of the German armoured forces, seem good.' Wavell would never have been so optimistic, yet on paper Auchinleck's assessment might have 71

seemed correct: the British tanks still held Sidi Rezegh and at
10.30 a.m. on the 22nd the 5th South African Brigade had begun to
move north, promising valuable reinforcement, while the New
Zealand Division infantrymen in 13th Corps were forcing up to the
west. But remaining armoured regiments in the 30th Corps at Sidi
Rezegh were already weak, and the contact between Cunningham
at the front and Auchinleck never achieved the almost instinctive
cohesion enjoyed by Rommel and Crüwell.

Already, as Auchinleck sent his confident report to London, the
German commanders were making bids for the initiative: during
the afternoon of the 22nd Crüwell thrust towards the eastern flank
of the 7th Armoured Division at Sidi Rezegh with the regrouped
15th Panzer, while Rommel improvised a brilliant flanking movement – infantry, artillery from 21st Panzer and tanks from 5th
Panzer Regiment slipped past Belhamed, made a wide turn, and
struck at Sidi Rezegh airfield from the west. The operation achieved
complete surprise and wrought havoc among the confused British
defenders. Tanks milled in the dust trying to fend off the unexpected
attack, and Gott had to order the 7th Armoured Division to fall
back south on to the approaching South Africans, leaving the *Afrika
Korps* in control of the central airfield area.

The battle became even more bewildering. 'It is just not possible
to tell precisely what is happening,' complained Captain Fielding.
'Distances are so great. Things move so quickly. Information is
hard to come by.' German and British units blundered into one
another, fought, veered off, chased and harried each other across
the ridges and dunes. At dusk on the 22nd 15th Panzer crashed into
the HQ of the British 4th Armoured Brigade and the 8th Hussars,
and the Germans switched on their head-lights and began to
round up prisoners. Conversely, New Zealand troops surprised the
Afrika Korps HQ at dawn on the 23rd, missing Crüwell but capturing
most of his staff and equipment. Both Rommel and Auchinleck tried
to keep grips on the fast-flowing situation.

'It looks as if the battle is moving to its climax,' signalled Auchinleck to London on the 23rd. Chaotic conflict continued during this
Sunday. Rommel attempted to deploy a pincer movement, but
orders failed to reach Crüwell until the afternoon, and Rommel
himself was out of reach for most of the day, probably trapped in the
swirling groups of tanks and infantry. Both British and German
subordinate commanders found they had to act largely independently from their superiors, using their own initiative. The New
Zealanders struggled in a bloody clash around the eastern end of the
main Sidi Rezegh ridge, and by nightfall had suffered 450 casualties,

Loading a drum cable,
to be taken forward in
preparation for battle.
Painted by Ivor
Beddoes.

Part of the gigantic
allied assault force
heading for French
North Africa in
operation 'Torch'.
Painted by Richard
Eurich.

their highest rate of loss so far including Greece and Crete; another New Zealand battalion managed to slip south towards the 5th South Africans below Sidi Rezegh. But these brave South Africans found themselves confronted by the full force of Crüwell's armour and motorised infantry, which had swept through the remains of the 7th Support Group – Campbell, still in command of the latter, tried to rally his men with 'Stop' and 'Go' flags made from his scarves, and at one time shouted to artillery troops: 'Stick to me! I shall advance soon!' Bravery shown by Campbell and his decimated units could not block the pounding German tanks; Crüwell plunged south-west, joined the *Ariete* division, formed up his armour and infantry, and then charged directly at the 5th South African Brigade. Almost seventy German tanks were destroyed, but the *Afrika Korps* slammed on, over the South African defences, and by nightfall the defenders had lost 3,394 men. Survivors continued to struggle. 'Twilight came,' wrote the German general Bayerlein, 'but the battle was still not over. Hundreds of burning vehicles, tanks and guns lit up the field . . .' Rommel, 'in a state of excited exultation', decided upon perhaps the boldest move of his whole North African campaign: success would bring him praise as a military genius; failure would mean complete condemnation.

The 'Desert Fox' would split his forces. One portion would stay to finish the battle at Sidi Rezegh; the other would strike far to the east, towards Egypt. By midnight on the 23rd he had relayed his decision to Berlin. 'Intention for 24 November. (a) To complete destruction of the 7th Armoured Division. (b) To advance with elements of forces towards Sidi Omar with a view to attacking enemy on Sollum front.' The plan to divide his army, amidst so much confusion, underlined Rommel's constant coolness and self-confidence, and his attitude contrasted sharply with that displayed by his opposing general. On this same day, 23 November, Cunningham lost his nerve. The 8th Army commander realised the British had suffered heavy tank losses, and feared the *Afrika Korps* might soon slaughter his exposed infantry divisions – and might be able to advance into Egypt. He asked Auchinleck to join him for urgent talks, and the British C-in-C reached the 8th Army HQ during the evening. Auchinleck listened to Cunningham's depressing assessment, then refused to consider calling off the offensive; the struggle must continue, declared Auchinleck, and he pointed out that the enemy must be as extended as his own forces. The War Cabinet therefore received a surprisingly optimistic signal on the 24th: 'The Germans are fighting with great tenacity and casualties on both sides are heavy. South of Tobruk the position is very confused, but

Opposite:
Men of the 2nd Bn.
The Rifle Brigade in the
vicious maul for Kidney
Ridge, El Alamein.
Painted by Terence
Cune.

77

Rommel viewing
operations from his staff
car (standing on the
right). During
'Crusader' the German
commander exposed
himself constantly to
enemy fire, moving
amongst his forward
troops to urge them on
and even to lead the
way. His personal staff
suffered injury and
death, but almost
miraculously the Desert
Fox continued to survive
unscathed.

we have gone a long way towards rolling up the enemy's frontier positions.' Churchill received another message from Auchinleck, now back in Cairo: 'I have decided to replace General Cunningham temporarily by General Ritchie, my present Deputy Chief of Staff ... I have reluctantly concluded that General Cunningham, admirable as he has been up to date, has now begun to think defensively, mainly because of our large tank losses.'

Meanwhile, Rommel had darted forward for Egypt on the 24th, aiming at severing the retreat of the 30th Corps and driving 13th Corps back on to the frontier minefields at Sollum. Rommel himself led the advance in his staff car; behind him came 15th Panzer and the *Ariete* Division, and although the Italians were blocked by the South Africans, the German tanks began to create havoc in the 30th Corps rear areas. Brigadier Clifton, Chief Engineer of the 30th Corps, described how 'almost unopposed, driving everything ahead like sheep, about twenty German tanks rolled eastwards, completely disintegrating our rear organisation'. During the evening of the 24th Crüwell managed to catch up with Rommel and received orders for the following day: to strike at the heart of the

78

13th Corps near the frontier wire. Crüwell expressed doubts: his supplies were extremely stretched and his tanks were suffering increased mechanical troubles; his men were exhausted. Rommel refused to accept any argument. Crüwell departed to deploy his weary forces – and Rommel narrowly escaped capture when he had to spend the night in a broken-down vehicle within yards of moving British trucks.

Tuesday, 25 March, was perhaps the most decisive day of the whole stubborn battle. The drive forward by Rommel – his famous 'dash to the wire' – apparently justified all the unease felt by Cunningham. But Auchinleck stayed calm, determined to maintain the offensive towards Tobruk; and his obstinacy, transmitted to the flagging army via General Ritchie, robbed Rommel of his victory. With the British still fighting doggedly in his rear, the Desert Fox found himself exposed. The *Ariete* division was unable to disengage from the South Africans, and Crüwell's attempt to smash through the 4th Indian Division failed. Rommel, under intense strain for the past week, temporarily lost control, acting in a totally uncharacteristic unsure fashion. The New Zealand Division had continued to push forward for Tobruk under the indomitable Freyberg, and by 26 November had almost achieved a junction with the garrison – despite appalling casualties.

> There was an enormous number of dead and wounded all over the battlefield [stated the New Zealand official historian]. A significant feature was the sight of many men who had been hit by solid shot of anti-tank guns fired at point-blank range. These projectiles had torn large portions of flesh from the bodies of their unfortunate victims and it would be hard to imagine a more unpleasant sight or a more heavily contested battlefield.

At the same time the battered British armoured units in the Sidi Rezegh area were taking advantage of Rommel's absence and were hastily reorganising. On 27 November, the day the first New Zealanders finally linked with the Tobruk garrison, Ritchie signalled Auchinleck: 'As I see it the major situation in Cyrenaica as a whole is excellent from our point of view and all indications are that the enemy is getting more and more hard put to it.'

The British seemed about to accomplish a full-scale junction with the still-powerful Tobruk garrison; reforming British armour lay astride the supply lines to the *Afrika Korps* formations up by the Egyptian frontier; Rommel remained out of touch with the position in the main battlefield area. The German situation seemed indeed desperate. But now an ordinary staff colonel, Westphal, acted with courage and determination to begin correcting the position. 79

Westphal, left in charge of the HQ near Tobruk, took it upon himself on the 27th to send a dramatic order to the 21st Panzer Division: 'these tanks must return from the Egyptian frontier and move west towards Tobruk, in the rear of the New Zealanders.' Ravenstein, commander of the 21st Panzer, thought the order came from Rommel and hastened to obey. The Desert Fox flew back to El Adem on the night of the 27th, where German staff officers waited apprehensively for his reaction to matters being virtually taken out of his hands. He stalked over to the maps, examined them, and said nothing; in fact he had already ordered the other main *Afrika Korps* unit, 15th Panzer, to return to El Adem after clearing up the situation around Sollum. The panzers had begun to concentrate again; Rommel's grip had come back. And even on the 27th, the day he flew back to his anxious officers at El Adem, he had found time amidst the dreadful turmoil to jot a letter to his wife: 'It's our 25th wedding anniversary today ... I want to thank you for all the love and kindness through the years which have passed so quickly; I think, with gratitude to you, of our son, who is a source of great pride ...' Still caked with dust, his eyes bloodshot and red-rimmed, his limbs leaden, Rommel issued his orders on the 28th: the New Zealand Brigade must be destroyed and the ring must be snapped tight around Tobruk.

For the next three days the fighting reached a new intensity on the scarred and smoking escarpments around El Duda, Belhamed and Sidi Rezegh. The battle for Tobruk reached an even more crucial stage. Sections of the battlefield changed hands repeatedly, but the New Zealanders continued to hold out almost against all odds. Von Ravenstein fell captive on the 29th and by this time the German forces were beginning to falter; 15th Panzer had been thrown back by the British armour and 21st Panzer seemed to be bleeding to death. Rommel urged his units forward again on the 30th despite the previous heavy losses: the 21st Panzer had only fifteen medium and six light tanks left, and 15th Panzer had only twenty-eight medium and eleven light, while the British 7th Armoured had 120 tanks of all types. But this British formation had veered away from the critical New Zealand positions to the southwest of Sidi Rezegh – and Freyberg's four battalions in his 6th Brigade could now muster only twenty-six officers and 829 men. During the afternoon 15th Panzer climbed up the escarpment and charged into the attack: within ninety minutes half the 6th New Zealand Brigade positions had been overrun with terrible casualties. Next day the 4th New Zealand Brigade was overwhelmed at

Belhamed after having lost five commanding officers in the previous three days – and Tobruk had again been isolated. German forces once more hovered at the port perimeter, ready to fend off renewed attempts by British armour to break through to the garrison. 'On paper we seemed to have won the "Crusader" battle,' wrote von Mellenthin on Rommel's staff. 'But the price paid was too heavy; the *Panzergruppe* had been worn down, and it soon became clear that only one course remained – a general retreat from Cyrenaica.'

Rommel had lost 142 of the 249 tanks with which he had started the battle. He had no reserves. Auchinleck was pushing more armour and more men at utmost speed to the desert front. Both sides were suffering from exhaustion, but the Germans fared worse, isolated at the end of their over-stretched supply lines. Few commanders would have disagreed with von Mellenthin's conclusion that the Germans must call off the battle and retreat. Rommel had different ideas. On 2 December he ordered the counter-attack.

Vicious fighting continued for another five days. Rommel threw his remaining tanks in one direction then another in an attempt to smash the British armoured units before they could be reinforced to an irresistible level. He took advantage of uncoordinated movements by the 30th Corps on 4 December to strike towards Bir el Gubi, only to have to pull back again when the *Afrika Korps* seemed in danger of a British outflanking movement. Next day Rommel tried again, stabbing south to seek a decisive engagement with the 7th Armoured, only to find himself blocked by the 11th Indian Brigade. RAF bombing intensified each day, and British artillery took a heavy toll, yet the *Afrika Korps* continued to struggle; tank crews and infantrymen on both sides were almost dropping with weariness and one fearful day merged into another.

> I can truthfully say [wrote an officer in the 3rd Royal Tanks] that none of us had more than the vaguest idea where we were from day to day and hour to hour, or what was happening either to our own forces or the enemy's ... There was no such thing as advance and retreat. We roared off to areas of threat or engagement depending on the urgency of the information. We chased mirages and were chased by mirages. Every few hours a landmark or a name would punch our memories with an elusive familiarity, and we would recall a forgotten early incident or a battle fought there days before that was now part of a past so near in time but so distant in event.
>
> We went without sleep, without food, without washing or change of clothes, without conversation beyond the clipped talk of wireless procedure and orders. In permanent need of everything civilised, we snatched greedily at everything we could find, getting neither enjoyment nor nourishment.
>
> The daily formula was nearly always the same – up at any time between midnight and 4 o'clock; movement out of the leaguer into

Rommel's tank casualties steadily increased. Here, a member of a knocked-out German tank crew surrenders as British infantry rush forward.

battle positions before first light; a biscuit and a spoonful of marmalade before the flap of orders and information; the long day of movement and vigil and encounter, death and the fear of death, until darkness put a limit to vision and purpose on both sides; the drawing in of far-flung formations; the final endurance of the black, close-linked march to the leaguer area; the maintenance and replenishment and order groups that lasted till midnight; the beginning of another twenty-four hours ...

On 7 December even Rommel had to admit defeat. At 9.30 a.m. he gave Crüwell his orders for the day '*Afrika Korps* was to hold out today and keep the enemy off, and to counter-attack if the enemy pressed too hard. During the night it was to withdraw thirty to thirty-five kilometres northwest.' Rommel would pull back to a prepared defensive line running south from Gazala. The German panzers retained their tight control and by the 12th had reached the Gazala line, but the reinforced 8th Army continued to press against the withdrawing units, and Rommel was obliged to take another painful decision. On 15 December he reported to Berlin: 'After four weeks of continuous and costly fighting ... the men are beginning to show signs of weariness, particularly as supplies of equipment and munitions have completely broken down ... Withdrawal, via El Mechili-Derna, during the night of 16/17 December at the latest, is unavoidable.' Already, on 4 December, Rommel had heard from Mussolini that apart from basic food and ammunition requirements, the *Afrika Korps* could expect no more supplies until early January;

82

the Desert Fox knew he would be unable to withstand British pressure for more than a few days, and despite vehement Italian protests his formations resumed their retirement on the night of the 16th. This time they pulled back at maximum speed; the British rushed after them. 'On and on and on we went,' wrote Captain Fielding in his diary on the 17th, 'the Brigade streaming out behind us like a huge armada of destroyers, each vehicle with its own little bow wave of dust and larger wake of churned-up sand.' By 22 December the Germans had withdrawn to Beda Fromm and Antelat, and the speed of their westward movement had dislocated Ritchie's plans for an enveloping pursuit, in addition to aggravating his problems of defective vehicles and flagging men. Rommel gradually neared his supply ports while the 8th Army now struggled at the end of a long line of communications; on 23 and 24 December the Germans pulled back into Agedabia. Final attempts by tanks of the 22nd Armoured Brigade to break through the German rear-guard failed on 28 December, and by the beginning of January 1942 the *Afrika Korps* had retired to the safety of Agheila. 'Crusader' finally spluttered to an exhausted end.

Auchinleck and Ritchie could claim the honours for the long and bloody battle, but victory brought fresh problems. The 8th Army now had to operate far from the new forward base at Tobruk; heavy losses suffered in 'Crusader' had to be replaced; units had to be reformed and reorganised. On 15 January Auchinleck had to accept an assessment by Ritchie that a renewed offensive could not be attempted before 11 February, and that Benghazi must first be built up as an advanced supply port. Moreover, tremendous events had happened elsewhere: the Japanese had swooped upon Pearl Harbour on 7 December, and although the Americans had been precipitated into the war the situation in the Far East seemed extremely precarious. Supplies destined for North Africa might have to be diverted. Britain suffered acute shipping shortages: the *Repulse* and *Prince of Wales* had been sunk in Malayan waters, and the Battle of the Atlantic had continued to take a deadly toll. Royal Naval strength in the Mediterranean had suffered through this over-stretch: on 4 January an Italian convoy had begun to cross the Mediterranean, and this reached Tripoli unhindered on the 5th; this success, believed Admiral Sir Andrew Cunningham, showed existing Royal Naval surface forces in the Mediterranean were now powerless to intercept enemy seaborne supplies, and maritime air-

British troops struggle over another ridge in the tumult of battle. In the foreground two ambulance men attend to a casualty.

craft were inadequate even for reconnaissance purposes – and he warned that Malta would probably soon be subjected to grossly intensified attack.

Troops in the desert struggled to reorganise themselves amidst the harsh winter weather. Men shivered around scrappy fires as the rain sheeted across the wilderness. 'It's cold, damp and pitch-black,' wrote Private Crimp. 'You can hear the dismal howling of jackals, now from this direction, now from that, and occasionally the maniacal gibbering of a hyena.' Desert conditions offered minimum chance of rest after the terrors of the recent battle, and shortages of supplies reduced the possibilities of obtaining even the simplest comforts.

> Everyone brassed-off. There's been no fag-issue for over a fortnight, nor any NAAFI supplies, due to transport difficulties (we're a long way forward from the dumps), and most chaps' reserves have run out. Ernie and Sam have even been reduced to drying tea-leaves and rolling them in newspaper …

In the German lines around Agheila men suffered similar discomfort, closer though they were to supplies. The *Africa Korps* had to be rebuilt. Mechanics toiled to assemble battle-worthy tanks from scraps of old – perhaps 380 had been lost out of 412 in the total eventually committed to the 'Crusader' struggle; new vehicles were hastily modified for desert conditions. Fresh recruits received intensive training. By mid-January the *Afrika Korps* had been supplied with about 100 new operational tanks, and gaps in the manpower ranks had been substantially filled, but the Germans still lacked aircraft – over eight hundred machines out of a thousand had been shot down in the previous two months.

Yet the Desert Fox had lost none of his daring. 'The situation is developing to our advantage,' he wrote to his wife on 17 January, 'and I'm full of plans that I daren't say anything about round here. They'd think me crazy. But I'm not; I simply see a bit farther than they do. But you know me.' Rommel spread rumours that the *Afrika Korps* intended a further withdrawal; the Italians heard the stories with consternation and the British with relieved satisfaction. On 20 January the whispers were apparently confirmed when houses in Marsa el Brega were blown, presumably to demolish stores which could not be taken with the retiring German army. But next morning, 21 January, German officers read this Order of the Day from Rommel: 'You have survived severe fighting against a greatly superior enemy. But your fighting spirit is unbroken. At this time we are numerically stronger than the enemy before us. To destroy them the Army will start to attack, today …'

Chapter 4

Retreat

'The improbable occurred,' wrote Auchinleck in his later despatch, 'and without warning the Axis forces began to advance.' Rommel's staff had given a valuable assessment to their commander on 12 January: the British were weak in front-line forces and for the next fortnight the Germans would have numerical superiority; thereafter the British would gain in relative strength. This precise appreciation proved correct: the 7th Armoured Division had been withdrawn to rest and refit, and its replacement, the 1st Armoured Division, was deficient by one brigade; moreover the men in this new formation lacked desert training. British units were widely dispersed and still suffered equipment shortages. The war against Japan had indeed sapped British strength in North Africa, with the transfer of men, equipment, aircraft and artillery, and the port of Benghazi had yet to be made viable. Rommel, always the opportunist, seized the temporary advantage: his forces would strike 'like greased lightning'. Two columns advanced on the 21st. One, codenamed Group Marcks and comprising elements of the 90th Light and 21st Panzer, drove down the coastal road, while the second advanced inland north of Wadi el Faregh. Almost immediately the surprised British forward units began to fall back, and sensing the possibility of creating panic, Rommel placed himself at the head of Group Marcks to press his panzers onwards to Agedabia.

General Ritchie was in Cairo when the attack began. Communications with the front seemed confused and reports reaching London from the Middle East HQ underestimated the threat. The War Cabinet, preoccupied with an imminent Japanese offensive against the woefully inadequate Singapore defences, were informed at 6 p.m. on the 22nd that 'General Rommel has delivered a counterstroke on Agedabia which might be no more than a reconnaissance in force, which has driven our outposts in about ten miles.' Ritchie reached the fighting during the afternoon of the 23rd and still believed the enemy to be attempting a strong reconnaissance: soon would come 'a God-sent opportunity to hit him really hard when he puts his neck out as it seems possible he may be already doing'. This optimism was echoed in a cable to Churchill from Auchinleck: 'If Rommel persists he is likely to expose his eastward flank to attack...' Yet the 8th Army continued to withdraw in increasing confusion throughout Saturday, 24 January, although managing to avoid an encircling attempt by the confident Rommel.

Heinz Schmidt, a tank commander, revealed one reason for the Axis success: 'We had now developed a new method of attack. With

Opposite 'I owe everything to my soldiers' – Rommel promoted to Field-Marshal.

87

our twelve anti-tank guns we leap-frogged from one vantage point to another, while our panzers, stationary and hull-down, if possible, provided protective fire. Then we would establish ourselves to give them protective fire while they swept on again … We could not help feeling that we were not then up against the tough and experienced opponents who had harried us so hard on the Trigh Capuzzo.' British units struggled to retain cohesion in the bewildering withdrawal. Sergeant Grey of the Camerons recorded one small but typical action in this extremely fluid fighting.

A large German jumped out from behind a bush and pinned me before I could think. A German and an Italian officer came running up, took my rifle and equipment off me, stuck automatics in my stomach and back, while the Italian, speaking perfect English, said: 'Lead us to your comrades; tell them to surrender and you will be well treated.' I feigned sickness and stupidity and asked for water, but got kicked in the stomach by the German. There seemed no alternative, so I pointed to my left … I started off up the hill, with the officers on either side, and stumbling in the dark managed to bring my platoon well on to my flank. Then I aimed for their position, which I could just distinguish in the dark. I heard a Jock say, 'Here the b—s come.' Then the Italian said: 'Shout to them to surrender!' So I shouted: 'McGeough, McGeough!' (I knew he was a good shot), got within ten yards of them, shouted 'Shoot!' and fell flat. The boys shot and got the German in the head and the Italian in the stomach. Grand! So off I ran and rejoined the platoon. By then we were long past our withdrawal time; so back

A derelict Italian lorry is hit by German bombers, pinpointing the British for further *Luftwaffe* attacks: a British anti-aircraft Bren gunner tries desperately to help with defence.

we went, and after a bit of bayonet work by the rear platoon, jumped into lorries and drove off with the Germans lining the road behind us, popping at us at pointblank range ...

During the afternoon of the 24th a further signal from Auchinleck revealed rising apprehension: 'Enemy has been able to maintain unexpected strength forward apparently, and his initial advance seems to have disconcerted temporarily at any rate our forward troops ... But his supply position this time is no way comparable with last year.' Some German officers agreed with Auchinleck's assessment of the Axis supply difficulties; Rommel refused to listen. 'We were not entirely happy about our petrol position,' remembered Schmidt. 'Yet one young officer, who said to Rommel, "Herr General, we need more fuel," received the brisk answer: "Well, go and get it from the British."' This the *Afrika Korps* proceeded to do.

In the early hours of Sunday, 25 January, a service signal from the naval liaison officer with the 8th Army to the C-in-C Mediterranean was passed to the Chiefs of Staff in London: preparations were being made to evacuate Benghazi, previously judged an essential British supply port, and the signal warned: 'Should Benghazi fall Derna will follow.' Churchill reacted with an anxious message to Auchinleck.

> I am much disturbed ... I had certainly never been led to suppose that such a situation could arise ... Have you really had a heavy defeat in the Antelat area? Has our fresh armour been unable to compete with the resuscitated German tanks? It seems to me this is a serious crisis, and one to me quite unexpected. Why should they all be off so quickly?

To find answers to Churchill's questions Auchinleck rushed forward to the 8th Army HQ on the 26th, but his arrival merely added to the confusion. Both Auchinleck and Ritchie remained optimistic, yet the field commanders were still pulling back before the intense German pressure. General A. Godwin-Austen, commander of 13th Corps, believed he might soon be encircled and ordered 4th Indian to pull out of Benghazi, while General Messervy, commander of the 1st Armoured, shifted back to Mechili. Auchinleck and Ritchie intervened to cancel this withdrawal; Rommel, intercepting the spate of wireless messages, seized on the British indecision – orders were given for a two-pronged attack, with forces striking along the northern coast road, and with Rommel himself leading Group Marcks through the hills to the south-east of Benghazi to attack from this entirely unexpected direction. At the same time, the *Afrika Korps* would feint towards Mechili to draw the enemy.

The Axis forces began their offensive on the 28th, with superb

A German bomb explodes close to a retreating British convoy.

success. Ritchie mistook the *Afrika Korps* deception as the spearhead for the main attack and believed Rommel had laid himself wide open; he therefore ordered 1st Armoured to move into a position near Mechili from which it could engage this 'main' German force – and yet the British tanks were urgently required to give support for the infantry at Benghazi. General Sir Francis Tuker, outspoken

commander of the 4th Indian at this port, anxiously awaited the
arrival of armour. 'We rang Army – and learnt to our consternation
that the whole of the eastern flank had gone off on a wild goose
chase after a phantom force of enemy armour falsely reported to be
moving on Mechili.' The despairing Tuker added: 'Dispersion,
dispersion and dispersion …' He insisted that Benghazi could not

be defended without armour, and Ritchie was forced to agree. Benghazi was evacuated. The Indian Division fled – straight into the arms of Rommel who had led his Group Marcks through the hills, pressing on despite harsh terrain and frequent rain squalls. Tuker managed to extricate the bulk of his men from the German mesh, but had to retreat as fast as he could. And at 10 a.m. on the 29th, amidst gentle spring sunshine which had replaced the showers, Rommel rode triumphantly into Benghazi. The shaken 8th Army pulled back to a defensive line south of Gazala, facing a thin frontage of *Afrika Korps* units; Rommel, once more short of supplies and fuel, had to regain his breath and had to keep his main forces further back. In seventeen days he had pushed the British almost to Tobruk, and had recovered much of the ground lost in the five-week 'Crusader' battles. The 1st Armoured Division had lost about three-quarters of its tank strength – nearly a hundred vehicles – plus about 1,000 prisoners and thirty-eight guns. The *Afrika Korps* had only suffered about thirty tank casualties.

The news caused intense depression in London, where it arrived during a time of peak anxiety for Singapore and while Churchill was defending his Government during a House of Commons Vote of Confidence debate. 'I offer no apologies. I offer no excuses. I make no promises ...' Next day, 29 January, Auchinleck cabled his assurance that the loss of Benghazi would only be temporary, but added: 'It must be admitted that the enemy has succeeded beyond his expectations and mine, and that his tactics have been skilful and bold.' Within twenty-four hours another cable from Auchinleck reached London: 'I am reluctantly compelled to conclusion that to meet German armoured forces with any reasonable hope of decisive success our armoured forces as at present equipped, organised and led must have at least two to one superiority.' Also on 31 January the Chiefs of Staff decided that plans for an allied landing in the French colonies of North Africa, 'Gymnast', discussed with the Americans over the previous month, must be shelved. All reinforcements should be rushed to the Far East. The battle for Singapore began eight days later and ended after one week of bitter fighting; Japanese forces now threatened Burma. Not since the grim days of early summer, 1940, had British fortunes sunk so low; never before had Churchill suffered so many setbacks. 'It was his darkest hour,' wrote General Sir Alan Brooke, now the Chief of the Imperial General Staff. 'The weight of his burden would have crushed any other man.'

The Prime Minister responded in typical fashion: he called for renewed action and increased effort regardless of crippling shortages

of equipment and manpower. An early offensive must be launched in the Western Desert, and the need for this campaign had been aggravated by the perilous position of Malta. Brooke warned the War Cabinet on 25 February that 'the situation in Malta would be critical, unless we could recapture Benghazi before May at the very latest', in order to secure advance airfields for air coverage of relief convoys. Churchill increased his pressure on Auchinleck. 'According to our figures,' he cabled Cairo on the 26th, 'you have substantial superiority in the air, in armour and in other forces ... The supply of Malta is causing us increasing anxiety ... Pray let me hear from you.'

Next day, 27 February, Auchinleck completed a gloomy 1,500 word appreciation which reached London at the start of March – and which, according to the official historian, 'raised a storm in Downing Street; the waters were not calm again until the end of March.' Churchill angrily summoned a Defence Committee meeting which began at 10 p.m. on 2 March; copies of Auchinleck's offending appreciation were spread on the table before the Ministers and the Chiefs of Staff. The Middle East Commander apparently refused to agree to a major desert offensive before June, despite the Chiefs of Staff insistence that an attack should be launched in mid-March or April to prevent a Maltese collapse. 'To

Men of a British Recovery crew fling themselves down as a German bomb explodes nearby. These Recovery units were especially valuable now, in early 1942, as both sides struggled to scrape together all available tanks.

93

launch a major offensive before then,' wrote Auchinleck, 'would be to risk defeat in detail and possibly endanger safety of Egypt.' He disagreed with Churchill concerning the degree of superiority required over the enemy and insisted he remained far too short in tank strength. The Prime Minister had already drafted a stinging reply to the Middle East Commander, which Brooke believed would only make matters worse. Admiral Sir Dudley Pound, First Sea Lord and Chairman of the Chiefs of Staff, hurriedly intervened at the meeting to say that 'the Chiefs of Staff were in agreement with the Prime Minister and were greatly disturbed ... They felt, however, that the first step should be the despatch from the COS of a telegram setting forth all the military arguments of the case.'

Lyttelton, who had returned from Egypt earlier in the day to become Minister of Production, with the Australian diplomat and politician Richard Casey taking over as Minister of State in Cairo, attempted to speak on Auchinleck's behalf. The reason for the C-in-C's 'cautious note', claimed Lyttelton, lay in the 'mechanical defects in their [the British] tanks and particularly to a failure in the cooling system ... The effect of this had been a loss of faith in equipment.' He continued:

> On top of this mechanical failure must be reckoned the superior gun position of the German tanks ... The Germans had developed a better form of tactic in the employment of their armoured formations; their tanks moved slowly from position to position waiting till they had discovered the location of our artillery and anti-tank weapons ... They kept out of the range of the latter and suffered little damage from the former.

Clement Attlee, Labour leader and Deputy Prime Minister in the wartime coalition, asked how Rommel could have mounted so successful a come-back in so short a time. 'Rommel had realised,' replied Lyttelton, 'as we did, that there were only two places in which to stand and fight in Cyrenaica, either right forward or right back.' Thus the Germans had pulled back causing overextension of the British lines, and then had taken advantage of superior gun-power and better mechanical efficiency to force the British to withdraw. Lyttelton continued to stress the loss of faith by 8th Army units in their equipment, and Brooke agreed that the tanks were indeed inadequate in some respects.

> Two defects had developed in the cruiser tanks, one in the fan-belt drive and one in the lubrication system. Nuffield engineers had been consulted and they said that they could rapidly fit modifications to a hundred tanks which would make them effective. The necessary spares and experts were being flown out.

94

Lyttelton commented that he had formed the impression 'that there was an imperfect liaison between the producer and the user'. Churchill declared he could not understand why the defects had not been noticed before. 'Surely every step should be taken to test out material before a battle, particularly as the fate of the whole campaign depended upon the reliability of the tanks. An inquiry on this point would be necessary.'

Discussion and argument continued until midnight, when the Defence Committee finally approved a cable to Auchinleck, already drafted by the COS, and invited Attlee to head the inquiry into the tank defects. The COS cable, dated 3 March, toned down Churchill's original angry draft, but nevertheless concluded:

> We consider that an attempt to drive the Germans out of Cyrenaica in the next few weeks is not only imperative for the safety of Malta on which so much depends, but holds out the only hope of fighting a battle while the enemy is still comparatively weak and short of resources.

The COS also criticised Auchinleck's assessment of relative strengths. Attlee would take almost three months to complete his requested inquiry, which would confirm most of Lyttelton's points – the tanks had been pressed into production before the pilot model had been adequately tested, and before defects had been detected and corrected.

Churchill, soon after the Defence Committee meeting on the 2nd, added his voice to the plea sent by the COS to Auchinleck on the 3rd. The C-in-C must bring forward his target date for the attack.

> We are agreed [signalled Churchill in his cable dated the 8th] that in spite of the risks you mention you would be right to attack the enemy and fight a major battle, if possible during May, and the sooner the better. We are prepared to take full responsibility for these general directions, leaving you the necessary latitude for their execution. In this you will no doubt have regard to the fact that the enemy may himself be planning to attack you early June.

Auchinleck retorted that the issue involved the question of whether, in the effort to save Malta, the whole British position in the Middle East would be jeopardised. Churchill immediately snapped back: 'I should be glad if you would come home for con-sultation at your earliest convenience.' Auchinleck refused to obey the Prime Minister's summons: in the present 'fluid' state of affairs, he cabled, it would be best if he remained on the spot. Churchill could do nothing, except relieve Auchinleck of his command, and this he hesitated to undertake; he merely told the intransigent commander that Sir Stafford Cripps, Lord Privy Seal, was about to leave on a mission to India and would stop in Cairo for discussions 95 on the 19th or 20th, where he would also be joined by General Sir Archibald Nye, the Vice-Chief of the Imperial General Staff. During this long-range duel between the two stubborn leaders, Malta received the full attention of the 160 *Luftwaffe* fighters and 250 bombers based on Sicily. The island refused to submit, and remained a threat to German supply lines into Egypt should the British be forced back from Gazala.

Yet the Maltese situation remained desperate. Four merchant ships left Alexandria on the 20th carrying urgent supplies for the island, totalling 26,000 tons. Two vessels were sunk during the passage and another was destroyed while being unloaded; only about five thousand tons were landed. Churchill's conviction of the need for an early North African offensive increased. But now the Prime Minister failed to obtain support from Cripps, who cabled that 8th Army strength remained insufficient to give reasonable chance of success, and an attack before mid-May would lead to unwarranted risk. 'I am very satisfied with the atmosphere at Cairo,' commented the Lord Privy Seal; he then escaped Churchill's wrath by hurrying on to India. General Nye in Cairo received a sarcastic signal from the Prime Minister on the 22nd:

> I have heard from the Lord Privy Seal. I do not wonder everything was so pleasant, considering you seem to have accepted everything they said, and all *we* have got to accept is the probable loss of Malta and the Army standing idle, while the Russians are resisting the German counter-strike desperately, and while the enemy is reinforcing himself in Libya faster than we are.

But Nye refused to be intimidated, sending a long and detailed report on the same day which also fully supported Auchinleck.

> If formations are to have 50 per cent reserve tanks it will only be possible by 15 May to equip two armoured brigades and two army tank battalions in addition to those now equipped . . . Considerations of training, both of armoured personnel and other arms . . . arise and limit the date by which these formations will be operationally ready even if tanks available.

Nye continued:

> C-in-C estimates that 50 per cent numerical superiority over German tanks and equality with Italian tanks necessary to give reasonable prospects of success . . . Probably number of tanks in possession of enemy by 15 May is admittedly a guess, but at worst may be 360 German and 312 Italian, which would require on C-in-C's estimate, 850 tanks of ours . . . It appears that at the very best we are not likely to have more than 500 tanks with formations in the forward area exclusive of reserves and I [infantry] tanks by 15 May.

The only conclusion to be drawn, added Nye, was that no offensive operations would be justified before 15 May.

The report received Defence Committee consideration on Thursday, 26 March, when Churchill still declared that he 'could not believe that we stood to gain on balance by postponing the offensive, even to the date mentioned by Auchinleck'. Sir Archibald Sinclair, Air Secretary, disagreed. 'The figures given in these telegrams made the chances of an early offensive appear slight.' Lyttelton continued to speak up for Auchinleck, declaring the C-in-C had recently changed the organisation of the armoured divisions and 'it would require a little time to train all formations in the new tactics'. Alexander, the First Lord of the Admiralty, sided with Churchill, but Auchinleck now had a powerful ally in Brooke. 'The period which would elapse before the offensive would make a great deal of difference in the state of our tanks and the training of our armoured formations. In addition, the railhead would have advanced to El Adem and this would ease the subsequent maintenance problem.' Churchill had to acquiesce: 'There seemed no alternative but to accept the date given by General Auchinleck.' A cable left the War Office agreeing to 15 May as the target date, yet within hours a signal bounced back from Cairo declaring that this target had been provisional on enemy tank strengths being less than the figure at present estimated for 15 May. 'C-in-Cs cannot bind themselves in any way to launch an offensive on 15 May in spite of the very obvious and urgent need.' Auchinleck and his naval and air colleagues were clearly determined to keep the initiative over Whitehall.

Likewise, Rommel prepared to win the initiative in the desert. At the end of April a meeting took place between Mussolini and Hitler at Obersalzberg, and from the discussions emerged a new directive for the Desert Fox: the *Afrika Korps* should launch an offensive against the Gazala Line as soon as possible, with Tobruk the target. After the capture of Tobruk the German forces in the desert would revert to the defensive while the main Axis effort shifted back to Malta. Rommel hurried to complete his plans and to take advantage of the increased flow of reinforcements to his base ports. Both sides therefore raced to be ready first. Each commander prayed that this time he would win the last, decisive battle. Troops trained for long hours in the desert heat, practising infantry assaults, tank manoeuvres and countless small exercises. The strain began to tell. Private Crimp wrote in his diary on 30 April:

This must undoubtedly be the most unpleasant time of the year in the desert, alternately hot and cold. It's the *Khamsin* season, and goes on   97 until mid-May. When the wind's from the north, it blows chilly and desolate, but when it's from the south, out of the Sahara, as today, it's far more disagreeable – dry, feverish, and suffocating.

Some units suffered from water shortage. 'The water position is bad,' commented Crimp, 'barely a gallon a day per man. Always thirsty.' He also wrote: 'Rations are very poor these days. For breakfast, a slice of bread and bacon; for lunch, half a slice of bread and tinned pilchards; for dinner, meat stew and potatoes, rice and prunes …'

Back over the desert in Cairo, Auchinleck, Ritchie and their staffs worked to meet the 15 May date – and found the task impossible. A cable from Auchinleck arrived in London on 7 May: the target settled so laboriously for the start of the offensive had been thrown back again, to at least 15 June. Auchinleck and his colleagues believed that to move earlier would incur risk of heavy tank losses and might bring only partial success, thus wasting all effort; a reversal would have disastrous consequences, opening the frontier of Egypt to a German advance. Moreover, even the 15 June date might have to be put back to August, should rumours of the imminent arrival of a new Italian armoured division prove correct. Brooke, summoned to the Prime Minister's bedside, found Churchill 'in one of his dangerous moods' insisting that Auchinleck must be replaced by General Alexander. Brooke confided in his diary that he feared Churchill 'might well take some wild decision', but the CIGS himself had been severely disturbed by the Cairo cable. Churchill took the matter to the War Cabinet next day, and informed Ministers that he had sent an interim reply to Cairo ordering plans to be continued for the 15 May date pending War Cabinet consideration. And so began another acrimonious exchange of cables between Ten Downing Street and Cairo, with Churchill and most of his Ministers insisting that the Middle East Command failed to realise the importance of Malta, and hence the need to secure forward air bases in the desert, and with Auchinleck, backed by the Middle East Defence Committee, daring to claim that the fall of the island need not necessarily be fatal to the security of Egypt, while the reverse would almost certainly be true.

Events in the desert rendered the argument irrelevant. On 19 May the Prime Minister received another signal from Auchinleck. 'There are strong signs that the enemy intends to attack us in the immediate future. If he does attack, our future action must be governed by the results of the battle and cannot be forecast now.' The signs were correct; next day, 20 May, Rommel issued his orders for the Axis offensive to begin on the night of the 26th.

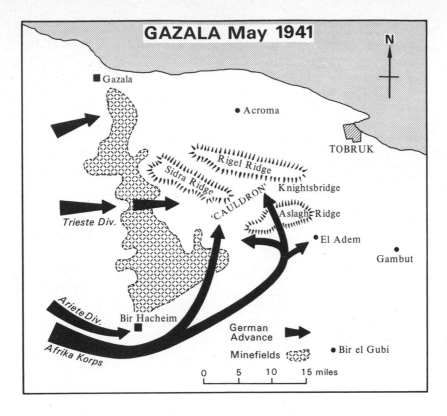

GAZALA May 1941

Gazala

Acroma

Rigel Ridge

Sidra Ridge

TOBRUK

Knightsbridge

'CAULDRON'

Trieste Div.

Aslagh Ridge

El Adem

Gambut

Ariete Div.

Bir Hacheim

German
Advance

Afrika Korps

Minefields

Bir el Gubi

0   5   10   15 miles

N

Also on the 20th Auchinleck sent a long message to Ritchie, assessing Rommel's likely moves: he believed an attempt would be made to smash through the central defence minefields while secondary forces feinted to the southern end of the British line at Bir Hacheim, and Auchinleck therefore warned Ritchie to concentrate the British armour in the centre. Ritchie on the other hand reckoned the enemy would probably sweep south of Bir Hacheim, while General Willoughby Norrie, commander of the 30th Corps, believed the primary German attack would come in the north along the coast. Rommel's actual orders contained a mixture of all three possibilities: his forces would feint in the north, a secondary attack would be made in the centre, and the main sweep would come in the south aiming first at Bir Hacheim. The latter thrust, led by Rommel, would consist of the *Afrika Korps*, now under General W. Nehring, plus the *Ariete* Division following close behind. The move south would start after dark on the 26th, and after overrunning the Free French defenders of Bir Hacheim the *Afrika Korps* would turn north behind the British line, while the *Trieste* Division made a frontal attack in the centre. Crüwell would lead German and Italian infantry in the northern feint, helped by the bulk of Rommel's 99

An advanced German
observation post. Fed by
reports from such posts
as this, Rommel pre-
pared his plan for the
offensive in May 1942.

artillery. The plan seemed simple and bold – too simple, because
Rommel had based his preparations on a number of misapprehen-
sions, chief among them being his lack of information concerning
Bir Hacheim. This French-held position would be the pivot of his
manoeuvre, and he believed he would be able to take it in as little as
an hour: he failed to appreciate the strength of the defence, and he
also believed the minefields ended well to the north of the fort.

    Rommel eagerly awaited battle, describing himself as in a state of
'high tension'. 'Dearest Lu,' he wrote to his wife on the 26th, 'by the

100

time you get this letter you will have long ago heard from the *Wehrmacht* communiques about events here. We're launching a decisive attack today.' Auchinleck had already received an encouraging signal from a magnanimous Churchill: 'We realise that success cannot be guaranteed. There are no safe battles … We have full confidence in you and your glorious army.' The Prime Minister had suggested Auchinleck should take personal command of the 8th Army, but Auchinleck had refused, replying that his place remained in Cairo. Ritchie, as always, enjoyed supreme optimism.

The Desert Fox began to advance late on the 26th aiming south-east for the sweep round the British desert flank.

> The move of this column of several thousand vehicles had been prepared in minute detail [wrote von Mellenthin]. Compass bearings, distances and speeds had been carefully calculated; dim lights concealed in petrol tins indicated the line of march, and with the smoothness of a well-oiled machine the regiments of the *Afrika Korps* swept on to their refuelling point south of Bir Hacheim.

At the last moment Rommel had given *Ariete* the task of taking Bir Hacheim, rather than the *Afrika Korps* which would push on to out-flank the position before striking north. Despite maximum efforts at secrecy the news of the German advance reached the 8th Army HQ during the night, but Rommel struck before the British could react. Ritchie had still to appreciate the primary factor of desert battles: the need to concentrate; 13th Corps in the north was split into a series of dispersed defensive boxes, while 30th Corps in the south, strengthened with the bulk of the armour, had been strung out in a succession of virtually isolated brigades. Rommel's massed tanks seized upon this dispersion. Early on the 27th his sweep overran the 3rd Indian Motor Brigade to the south-east of Bir Hacheim and then smashed into the 4th Armoured Brigade, which fell back to El Adem. Further to the east Rommel's 90th Light had surprised the 7th Motor Brigade. British positions lay wrecked, covered with burning vehicles, bodies and wounded, and a thick pall of smoke hung over the defences. At midday on the 27th, reported von Mellenthin, 'Rommel thought that the battle was won'.

But by evening the Desert Fox had been forced to change his assessment. Events were turning against him. Crüwell's feint in the north had failed to divert a significant number of British forces, and in the centre the *Trieste* division had become entangled in the mine-fields while 8th Army units had now reacted vigorously to the threat in the south. Rommel had severely underestimated the strength of the opposition, especially the power and efficiency of the new Grant tanks received from America with the 75-mm guns and 6-pounder 101

anti-tank weapons. 'The advent of the new American tank had torn great holes in our ranks,' commented Rommel. The 90th Light, pushing to the east, had become separated from the rest of the *Afrika Korps*, and above all the *Ariete* had failed to take Bir Hacheim, with this fort presenting an acute threat to Rommel's supply link as he attempted to move up behind the British lines. 'British motorised groups were streaming through the open gap and hunting down the transport columns which had lost touch with the main body,' reported Rommel. 'And on these columns the life of my army depended.' He added: 'It was clear that our plan to overrun the British forces behind the Gazala line had not succeeded.' Back in Cairo and far away in London the situation seemed confused, as usual, but nonetheless hopeful.

Despite the setbacks, Rommel remained confident as night fell on the 27th. 'I looked forward that evening full of hope to what the battle might bring.' His optimism stemmed from the tactics which

British AA gunners race to their weapon as the German offensive begins.

Ritchie was using against him. 'Ritchie had thrown his armour into the battle piecemeal and had thus given us the chance of engaging them on each separate occasion with just about enough of our own tanks. This dispersal of the British armoured brigades was incomprehensible.'

The 'penny-packet' method, originating from the deployment of the armour in separate defensive groups, continued to be used by the British on the 28th and reduced the benefits to be gained from the new Grant tanks. Rommel therefore continued to strike north behind Bir Hacheim, plunging into the smaller British formations which rushed to oppose him. Colonel G. P. B. Roberts, commanding the 3rd Royal Tanks, described one typical action south of El Adem. His regiment, part of the 4th Armoured Brigade, became entangled with much larger German forces.

There they are – more than a hundred. Yes, twenty in the first line, and there are six, no, eight lines, and more behind that in the distance; a

whole ruddy Panzer Division is quite obviously in front of us. Damn it. This was not the plan at all – where the hell are the rest of the Brigade? However, no indecision is possible because no alternatives present themselves ... The leading tanks had halted about 1,300 yards away; all our tanks were firing, there was no scarcity of targets, certainly two of our tanks were knocked out, but the enemy had also had losses. I could see one tank burning, and another slewed round and the crew 'baling out' ... 'Peter (my adjutant), tell Brigade we are holding our own but I do not anticipate being able to stay here for ever ... Peter, tell Brigade we cannot hang on here much longer, either there will be nothing left, or we will be cut off, or both. Driver, advance slightly into line with the other tanks. 75 gunner, enemy tank straight ahead receiving no attention – engage. First shot over – come down half-a-tank height. Still over – come down a whole tank's height. Good shot – that got him – same again.' Hullo! There is a dashing Boche on our left, he has come forward against C Squadron who have withdrawn a little, just the job for the 37-mm. '37 gunner, traverse left, traverse left, traverse left – on; enemy tank broadside – 500 – fire. 37 gunner – good – have a couple more shots ...'

In this fight Roberts' two squadrons of Grants were reduced to ten vehicles, in three of which the guns were out of action, and all ammunition had been used.

Similar engagements took place throughout the 28th as Rommel disregarded his tenuous supply lines and continued to move north.

Battle lasted deep into the night between 2nd and 22nd Armoured Brigades and the *Afrika Korps*, but by now Rommel had battered his way to the area behind the Gazala Line known as the Knights-bridge Box; the *Trieste* Division had continued to work through the central minefields; British armour had suffered heavily, although *Afrika Korps* losses were also considerable. Ritchie remained confident. But Rommel still retained the initiative: on the night of the 28th he ordered *Afrika Korps* to concentrate as soon as possible, and throughout the 29th his forces, scattered in previous engagements, gathered together again in the area between the Sidra and Aslagh ridges – to be known thereafter as 'The Cauldron'. Late on the 29th this vital concentration had been completed, and Rommel's latest orders revealed his brilliant plan: his *Afrika Korps* would fend off British armour while the Italians continued to work through the minefield to join the German tanks from the west. The British mines would themselves help protect his position. Once a gap had been gouged through the Gazala Line, Bir Hacheim to the south would be isolated – 'I intended to pinch out Bir Hacheim' – and after the fort had fallen Rommel could completely overturn the 8th Army position.

Fighting simmered in the Cauldron for another ten terrible days, with the massed German tanks blocking British counter-attacks, while the Free French clung to Bir Hacheim. These gallant defenders provided Rommel with perhaps his toughest opposition so far. 'I frequently took over command of the assault forces myself,' he wrote, 'and seldom in Africa was I given such a hard-fought struggle.' Day after day German artillery and aircraft blasted the smoking, reeking defences, and it seemed the French would never submit. But further north the *Afrika Korps* proved equally stubborn: a British counter-attack failed in the Cauldron on the night of 4 June, with the 8th Army tanks suffering ghastly casualties as they advanced across the open to the excellent German defences. 'Never for a moment did the [German] shelling stop,' declared the Royal Artillery historian. 'Casualties became heavier and heavier. Vehicles were burning everywhere. The enemy with their guns out of sight could direct their fire with great accuracy on the mass of men and vehicles and guns in the Cauldron below.'

One by one the British formations were destroyed.

The survivors of 426th Battery turned sadly to their final task – the battering of their gun sights. For a few moments more the air sang with machine-gun bullets; then all was quiet, and that deep silence that descends on a battlefield when the contest is over spread over the Cauldron.

Wounded British troops whose transport has struck enemy mines are being carried away on stretchers.

The last British units which could have blocked the Italian move through the central minefield, 150th Brigade, had already been eliminated.

Help did not arrive. At first light on 1 June the enemy attacked from all sides, and platoon by platoon the brigade was overrun and captured. The last sub-unit to go down was believed to be the platoon of the 5th Green Howards commanded by Captain Bert Dennis.

With the minefield gap completed and with the British counter-attacks beaten back in the Cauldron, Rommel could give added strength to the assault on Bir Hacheim. His tank and infantry losses had been heavy, but all available forces were now concentrated on the Free French, while from 7 June onwards the *Luftwaffe* attacked unceasingly from the sky. On 8 June, Crimp's diary entry revealed the rising anxiety being felt by the British. 'The Stukas are still

A British oil tanker burning in Tobruk harbour after a *Luftwaffe* attack.

dropping masses of muck. Rumour suggests the situation inside is getting a bit desperate. But why can't Jerry's grip be broken?' On 9 June the War Cabinet in London could still wring some hope from the Cairo reports. 'The German forces are about where they were at the beginning of the week,' Ministers were told, 'and must have suffered heavy casualties.' The 8th Army might still be able to shatter Rommel's prolonged attempt. But Private Crimp, among those who were attempting to sneak supplies in to the French, knew better. 'Tonight is the end of Bir Hacheim,' he wrote on the 10th. The surviving Frenchmen tried to break through during darkness.

> Soon after 10 o'clock the sharp rattle of an M/G burst is heard, and from now on it's bedlam: rat-tatting of machine-guns, crashing mortars, hoarse rumbling of shells, white, red and green lights climbing at all angles into the sky, streams of white and yellow tracer playing over the horizon, sprouting red glows and all the while the drone and surge of vehicle engines.

About 2,700 men including 200 wounded, out of the original 3,600, managed to get away. Crimp described their arrival:

> When there's sufficient light, single men and small bands approach furtively, and recognising, join us. They're haggard, unshaven, tattered and tired, but one after another, on the instinct of discipline, gripping weapons and equipment, they fall into rank. Some are quite young, others hardened old legionnaires. One youth, numb with fatigue, begs his warrant-officer for permission to go back for his rifle which he lost when his truck was hit.

108

'Now our forces were free,' commented Rommel. 'On the after-noon of 11 June, I put the Bir Hacheim force on the move to the north in order to seek a final decision without delay.' The main attack would be launched towards El Adem using 15th Panzer, 90th Light and *Trieste*, while 21st Panzer and *Ariete* feinted due north from Sidra to divert British forces in the Knightsbridge area. Enemy tanks were off the leash. By the evening of the 11th Rommel had reached El Adem and the British had been thrown disastrously off-balance. On the morning of the 12th Rommel created another of his devastating pincer movements, ordering 15th Panzer to attack the 2nd and 4th Armoured Brigades from the south, while 21st Panzer stabbed from behind. The Desert Fox remained in the thick of the fight, as always; on the opposing side Ritchie increasingly feared that the enemy might soon be able to cut off the infantry divisions in the north. All depended on the position at Knightsbridge in the centre, and especially upon the dominating Rigel ridge.

Rommel's orders for the 13th were for the pincer arms to con-verge; first *Afrika Korps* attacks were beaten off, but the enemy wheeled and charged again in the late afternoon, and the Scots Guards on Rigel ridge called for urgent help; once more the tanks battered forward, guns blazing through the shroud created by a fierce dust-storm and urged on by Rommel himself. Gradually the Scots Guards were prised from the escarpment and British tanks attempting to give support suffered heavy losses: 22nd Armoured Brigade had lost 105 heavy tanks out of about 150 and thirty-three out of about thirty-five light tanks during the past two days. Rommel's armour crashed to the summit of the ridge; the Desert Fox paid tribute to the Scots Guards defenders.

> This brigade was almost a living embodiment of the virtues and faults of the British soldier – tremendous courage and tenacity combined with a rigid lack of mobility. The greater part of the armoured force attached to the Guards Brigade was destroyed, either during that day or on their retreat the following night.

By the evening of the 13th Rommel had achieved an armoured superiority of about two to one, together with control of the central battlefield. Once more he turned his attention to Tobruk.

Ritchie had now to avoid encirclement and destruction of his decimated army. At 11.30 a.m. on the 14th he announced his decision 'to withdraw to the frontier and occupy the frontier de-fences,' even though he added that Rommel would be delayed as long as possible at El Adem and before Tobruk. He told Auchinleck at 11.10 p.m. that Tobruk should be abandoned for the time being.   109

But within an hour he received a directive from the C-in-C, issued earlier in the evening, which clashed with his plans: the enemy must not be allowed to use the Acroma–El Adem–Bir el Gubi approach to Tobruk, and British forces must counter-attack as soon as possible. Confusion between Cairo and the 8th Army HQ was reflected in signals to and from London. 'To what position does Ritchie want to withdraw?' cabled Churchill on the 14th. 'Presume there is no question in any case of giving up Tobruk.'

As usual, Rommel soon guessed this lack of cohesion on the part of the British, and made use of it. 'Full speed ahead was ordered, as British vehicles were now streaming east in their thousands. I rode with the tanks and constantly urged their commanders to keep the speed up . . .' And he wrote to his wife on the 15th: 'The battle has been won and the enemy is breaking up. We're mopping up encircled remnants of their army. I needn't tell you how delighted I am. We've made a pretty clean sweep this time.' His letter showed some exaggeration; the bulk of the 8th Army had escaped to the east. But these surviving elements were falling back in disorder, and Rommel continued to strike hard and fast. The *Afrika Korps*, with *Ariete*, was instructed to thrust for Gambut and its vital airfield. 'We wanted to divert British attention from Tobruk, and at the same time gain the necessary freedom of movement in our rear for the Tobruk attack. Primarily, however, this advance was directed against the RAF.' The 4th Armoured Brigade, now merely a patchwork of semi-units, clashed with 15th and 21st Panzer on the afternoon of the 17th, and by evening had suffered another heavy defeat. Also during the evening, Gambut fell. Rommel would be able to enjoy air superiority over Tobruk and the only possible relieving force for the garrison, 4th Armoured, had been shattered. Rommel poised his forces for the attack.

Even on the 19th, some optimism could still be felt at the Cairo HQ. Auchinleck and his colleagues completed an appreciation, despatched to London on the 20th, which declared: 'We hope ... that Tobruk should be able to hold out until operations for relief are successfully completed after resumption of our offensive.' Forty-eight hours before, Churchill had boarded a flying-boat at Stranraer for a cross-Atlantic flight to Washington. Dressed in his famous siren-suit, slippers and rakish black Homberg hat, twirling a gold-topped malacca cane, he had seemed almost elated. 'PM is in tremendous form,' wrote Brooke, 'and enjoying himself like a schoolboy.' Churchill had apparently no fears for Tobruk; capture of the port was unthinkable.

At 5.20 a.m. on the 20th the *Luftwaffe* droned over the besieged

Tobruk garrison and bombs blasted the defences in a pre-assault bombardment; by 7.45 a.m. the vital anti-tank ditch had been bridged and German tanks were nosing forward. The Australians in the perimeter had insufficient weapons, manpower and above all air cover. Within hours, grim signals were being received in London.

> Enemy attacked south-east face of Tobruk perimeter early morning after air bombardment and penetrated defences [declared Auchinleck in a cable dated the 20th and received at 1.15 p.m. on the 21st]. By evening all our tanks reported knocked out and half our guns lost . . . Major-General Klopper commanding troops in Tobruk last night asked authority to fight his way out feeling apparently could not repeat not hold out. Ritchie agreed … Do not repeat not know how he proposes to do this and consider chances of success doubtful …

At 3.05 p.m. on the 21st a telegram was relayed from Malta, where a signal had been received from Cairo: 'Critical situation rapidly developing on Libyan front … must ask you to despatch forthwith twenty Spitfires.' Two hours later a cable arrived in London from Casey, Minister of State in Cairo, immediately transmitted to Washington:

> You will receive a telegram almost at once from the Middle East Defence Committee telling you grave news that Tobruk has virtually fallen, and that it is proposed to fight as strong delaying action as possible on the positions on the Egyptian border in the vicinity of Sollum, but that the C-in-Cs believe the main stand cannot be made elsewhere than at Matruh … forces at our command in this theatre are inadequate to enable us to cope with the enemy.

Now, standing in the President's study in the White House, Churchill received 'one of the heaviest blows I can recall during the war'. An aide hurried in with a message; Roosevelt glanced at the pink slip of paper, then handed it in silence to the Prime Minister, who read the words: 'Tobruk has surrendered with 25,000 men taken prisoner.' For the first and only time in the war, Ismay noticed Churchill wince.

Chapter 5

Prelude to
Alamein

Rommel approached the doorway to Egypt. On the day he conquered Tobruk he received his promotion to Field-Marshal, and merely commented: 'I owe everything to my soldiers.' His leading units were rushing towards the frontier, while the main body of the fleeing 8th Army had tumbled back to Mersa Matruh, over fifty miles beyond the border, and the path of retreat lay strewn with abandoned equipment and broken vehicles. In Washington, the Americans made an immediate offer to Churchill of 300 precious Sherman tanks, 100 self-propelled 105-mm guns and air reinforcements; this aid would be of vital importance at El Alamein, but could do nothing to help prevent immediate disaster. Nor could recriminations and the search for scapegoats, yet Churchill insisted upon some sort of inquiry and telephoned London requesting an urgent War Cabinet meeting.

Ernest Bevin, Minister of Labour, attacked Auchinleck's handling of the situation: 'We should not tolerate the suggestion that Rommel and his troops were superior to our own ... Nevertheless, we now seemed to be witnessing the defeat of our forces in detail,' and he asked: 'Should not changes in the higher command be made?' Lyttelton reminded the War Cabinet that 'when General Auchinleck had been urged two months ago to stage an offensive in Cyrenaica, he had constantly affirmed that he was too weak in armour to do so with any prospect of success. Recent events might well confirm the correctness of this view.' Lyttelton added: 'The position on the frontier would not be restored by changes in the higher command.' Nevertheless he joined other Ministers in questioning the wisdom of only leaving a rearguard to hold the actual frontier while the main 8th Army remnants retreated back to Matruh. General Nye, Vice-CIGS, politely hinted that the War Cabinet should leave such matters to the commanders on the spot. 'The orders had already been issued ... This decision had been taken by the C-in-Cs, in consultation with the Minister of State and in possession of all the relevant factors, including the condition of their own troops.' Nye said he agreed with the policy of pulling back to Matruh. 'We should gain the advantage of fighting Rommel's armour 125 miles further from their base and of gaining time in which to assemble more armour for ourselves.' The War Cabinet agreed the decision could not be reversed from London, yet refused to abdicate all power of interference: a telegram would be sent to Cairo stressing the importance of a protracted defence of the frontier.

Opposite Scots Guards man hastily dug trenches in the latest and last British defensive positions – at El Alamein.

'I was determined at all costs,' wrote Rommel, 'to avoid giving the British any opportunity of creating a new front and occupying it with fresh formations.' His leading tanks brushed aside frontier defences on 23 June, and the main *Afrika Korps* pressed on in three columns towards Mersa Matruh. Churchill tried to boost morale; on the 25th he signalled Auchinleck: 'Whatever views I may have had about how the battle was fought or whether it should have been fought a good deal earlier, you have my entire confidence and I share your responsibilities to the full.' Next day, 26 June, Rommel had begun to threaten the makeshift opposition at Matruh. His plunging advance had given the British insufficient time to prepare adequate defences. Ritchie had frantically thrown New Zealand and Australian troops into a defensive line, which in fact was stronger on the flanks than in the centre. Rommel struck hard in the centre during the afternoon of the 26th, and thus inadvertently allowed the chance of a British pincer movement from the stronger flanks. But the British were still off-balance, while the Germans had kept the momentum of their advance, and by the evening of the 27th Rommel's 90th Light had broken through to sever the coast road to the east of Matruh, threatening the British rear. Once again 8th Army formations fell back in confusion, with 13th Corps breaking eastwards during the night of the 27th.

Auchinleck had taken over direct command of the 8th Army from Ritchie on the 25th, before the fighting at Mersa Matruh but too late to alter defensive plans. Nor had he time to influence the outcome of the battle. But his personality would soon be felt, with his confidence and calmness seeping through the 8th Army despite a situation verging on the catastrophic. By the time the 10th Corps had fallen back from Matruh on the night of the 28th, 30th Corps was already being organised in the next defensive positions less than fifty miles to the rear – at El Alamein. These defences would be unlike others previously held by the 8th Army: the accent would be on attack. Units would not be tied to a continuous belt of defended positions, nor would they be thrown piecemeal into haphazard assault. Instead, Auchinleck stressed the importance of fluidity. Divisions were to form mobile brigade battle groups, attacking the enemy with all available artillery concentrated at decisive points, and these battle columns would be firmly integrated into a cohesive whole; precious tanks would not be committed unless opportunities were judged extremely favourable, and infantry units would not be placed in isolated positions. Auchinleck ordered all units, men and material which could not be carried in allocated transport to be evacuated to the rear. Mobility must be

predominant, combined with a sense of balance which only a great commander could obtain – and Auchinleck, like Rommel, possessed this ability.

British tanks hurry into battered Mersa Matruh.

The difference in the 8th Army would soon be noticeable. Meanwhile, outside the battle area anxiety and elation mushroomed in the respective European capitals. Mussolini left for North Africa on 29 June to be on hand for a triumphant entry into Cairo. Eden told the War Cabinet at 5.30 p.m. on this Monday that the British Ambassador at Cairo had inquired 'whether arrangements should be made for evacuating civilian personnel', and the War Cabinet agreed the Ambassador should discuss matters with Casey, the Minister of State. Next day General George Marshall, US Chief of Staff, warned President Roosevelt that Rommel might reach the Suez Canal within a fortnight. Alamein lay merely sixty miles from Alexandria, and Churchill cabled to Casey: 'Everybody in uniform must fight exactly as they would if Kent or Sussex were invaded ... Egypt must be held at all costs.' Early next morning, 1 July, Rommel ordered his forces forward against El Alamein.

Rommel planned to drive 90th Light and the *Afrika Korps* south of Alamein and north of Deir el Abyad, after which the 90th Light would swing north for the coast, cutting off the British around Alamein while the *Afrika Korps* swept right to isolate 13th Corps. But by afternoon of 1 July the plan had started to slip astray. Rommel, in his haste to maintain the momentum of the advance, had undertaken insufficient reconnaissance and failed to realise the presence of the 1st South African division deployed in an excellent position to block 90th Light from turning north; likewise a new brigade, 18th Indian, lay to the east of Deir el Abyad in the path of the *Afrika Korps*. The South Africans reacted vigorously to the threat.

> Our troops were pinned down in terrific artillery fire [wrote Rommel]. An SOS came in from 90th Light ... I at once ... drove up myself in an armoured car to get a view of the situation and make my decisions. However, heavy British artillery fire soon forced us to turn back.

He tried again later in the day, hurrying forward urgent reinforcements.

> British shells came screaming in from three directions, north, east and south; anti-aircraft tracer streaked through our force. Under this tremendous weight of fire, our attack came to a standstill. Hastily we scattered our vehicles and took cover, as shell after shell crashed into the area we were holding. For two hours Bayerlein and I had to lie out in the open.

'Our troops were pinned down in terrific artillery fire,' wrote Rommel. Now, at the first push against the British defensive positions at Alamein, he found opposition had suddenly stiffened.

Further south the 18th Indian Brigade proved as stubborn as the South Africans. These Indians were newcomers: two of the three battalions had never seen action, and they lacked ammunition,

A sentry stands guard outside Cairo: Mussolini now planned to make a triumphant entry into the city after Rommel's desert victory.

artillery and armoured support. By the evening the brigade had been destroyed. But vital time had been gained, and so courage-ously did they cling to the ground on which they stood that Rommel thought these troops must be of divisional strength. Both sides stayed locked in combat on 2 July; neither had sufficient strength to obtain the advantage. Auchinleck's battle groups fought with new-found determination, yet lacked the equipment and training to make full use of this type of deployment. The C-in-C himself realised his forces were without sufficient punch to 'drive home an attack against anything but very weak resistance'; on the other hand Rommel's formations found that the 8th Army tanks now stood firm, drawing the enemy upon them with methods used by the *Afrika Korps* itself, rather than rushing out in all directions.

Cautious reports coming from the battlefield did nothing to relieve the anxiety in Cairo and in London. Ministers meeting at

Ten Downing Street at noon on 3 July heard a gloomy Chiefs of Staff report on 'what might happen if our forces were driven out of Egypt', with the COS believing the Germans intended to push over the Suez Canal to take Palestine and Syria, thus isolating Turkey and threatening Britain's vital oil supplies. Brooke described preparations for demolition work in Egypt, and Eden proposed to instruct the British Ambassador at Cairo to arrange civilian evacuation plans, although British civilians should 'stand fast' for the moment and preparations to leave should be kept hidden from the local population. The Prime Minister wanted to fly to Egypt; Brooke was dismayed: nothing would be worse than Churchill descending in mid-battle, and the CIGS spent almost an hour successfully arguing with him during the evening.

In Cairo itself, panic had reached dangerous proportions. Secret papers were being burnt, and the leading Egyptians were convinced that Axis tanks might soon be squealing down the streets. Private Crimp, returning to the desert after a short leave, witnessed one aspect of the situation.

> The road back from the western desert, where it turns south and traverses the fringe of the lake, is one big traffic jam … Down in the sidings at the bottom of the camp, a train loaded with NAAFI goods destined for the Front is being ransacked. Scores of squaddies are climbing into the wagons and helping themselves to as many bottles of beer, bars of chocolate and packets of biscuits as they can carry …

But on 3 July, while London, Cairo and Alexandria still rippled with apprehension, the scale had begun to tilt in the Western Desert. Almost unbelievably, Rommel had started to let slip the initiative which he had enjoyed since the ending of 'Crusader'. Private Crimp gave a hint in his diary of one reason: 'All along the desert road newly pitched airfields are in a state of great activity, formations of bombers and fighters continually taking off and flying westward'. The Desert Air Force had reached peak effectiveness: on 3 July the RAF flew 900 sorties against the Axis troops, about four times more than the *Luftwaffe* managed to undertake against the 8th Army, and in desert war control of the air would always be vital. This British supremacy in turn pointed to another advantage: the RAF were operating close to their airfields, while the *Luftwaffe* had far to go from base, and this applied to the overall question of supply – never before had Rommel's communications been so extended, and he had lacked sufficient time to bring forward essential stocks of equipment and ammunition.

By 3 July the *Afrika Korps* had only twenty-six tanks available for action, while the combined strength of 4th and 22nd Armoured

One of Rommel's tank
casualties being in-
spected by a British
soldier. A dead German
lies ignored in the
foreground.

The RAF achieve
supremacy in the desert
– a vital ingredient for
ultimate victory. Here a
British armoured car
reaches the German
victim of a dogfight.

Brigades totalled over 100, and by the end of the day Rommel's divisions had been reduced to 1,200 men. His troops were exhausted after their long advance, and the setback at the start of the First Battle of Alamein had taken away the elation of previous victories. This especially applied to the Italians: they had believed the gates of Alexandria and Cairo had been burst open; Auchinleck's stand had shown otherwise, and Axis morale began to collapse under the strain. During the 3rd the New Zealanders attacked the *Ariete* Division, overrunning part of this Italian sector and capturing 350 prisoners and forty-four guns. Rommel admitted: 'The Italians were no longer equal to the very great demands being made of them.' Auchinleck seized on this weakness, and from now on he would make special efforts to concentrate upon Rommel's faltering ally. The Desert Fox desperately needed time to regroup his armour and bring up reinforcements, and during the reorganisation would have to rely upon Italian infantry to fend off British probes; yet Auchinleck, despite the weariness of his own men, gave Rommel no chance to gain breath.

No longer could the Desert Fox hope for immediate victory, and on 4 July he had to admit to the German High Command that he 'expected to have to remain on the defensive for at least a fortnight'. Such a defensive stance, at the end of a long supply line and with the RAF predominant, would be extremely precarious, as Rommel well knew. Auchinleck therefore regained the initiative. Now the Germans, rather than the British, were thrown off-balance. 'I was compelled,' wrote a despairing Rommel, 'to order every last German soldier out of his tent or rest camp up at the front, for, in the face of the virtual default of a large proportion of our Italian fighting power, the situation was beginning to take on crisis proportions.' And he added: 'We finally had to give up all idea of fighting it out with the British in the Alamein line – the front had now grown static, and the British command was in its element.' He realised that this 8th Army leadership lay in the hands of a skilled and decisive general. 'Auchinleck was handling his forces with very considerable skill and tactically better than Ritchie had done. He seemed to view the situation with decided coolness, for he was not allowing himself to be rushed into accepting a second best solution by any moves we made.'

The British commander exerted pressure throughout July, first against the Italians in one sector, then another. Each day proved agonising for both attackers and defenders: the ruthless sun beat down, the flies swarmed black upon the faces of the living and the swollen dead, men almost came to blows as they struggled to slake thirsts from inadequate water supplies, their clothes were filthy and stank of sweat and petrol fumes, and desert sores festered upon their bodies. Auchinleck had taken over with a firm intention of altering the whole atmosphere in the 8th Army: 'These damn British have been taught far too long to be good losers. I've never been a good loser. I'm going to win.' But the total transformation of the 8th Army would take time. Attacks, although more efficiently planned than previously, often turned out muddled and wasteful as the battle dragged on; the middle strata of command between Auchinleck and his weary troops frequently proved unable to translate his intentions into reality. Yet the tide continued to turn. Liddell Hart summed up the situation at the end of July:

> The difference in total loss on either side was not large – and Rommel was not able to afford the loss. His account makes clear how perilously close he was to defeat in July. Moreover, his frustration in itself was fatal.

The Desert Fox had been forced to rush his forces from one threatened sector to another, day after day; by the beginning of August even he approached the end of his endurance.

Dirty and demoralised Italian prisoners line up for food and water. Auchinleck now made these doubtful allies of Rommel his prime target.

A well camouflaged
British gun helps
maintain pressure on
Rommel's extended
forces.

I'm thankful for evey day's respite we get [he wrote to his wife on
the 2nd]. A lot of sickness. Unfortunately many of the older officers are
going down now. Even I am feeling very tired and limp ... Holding on
to our Alamein position has given us the severest fighting we've yet seen
in Africa. We've all got heat diarrhoea now, but it's bearable. A year
ago I had jaundice and that was much worse.

This letter, above all else, is a tribute to Auchinleck's rescue of the
8th Army; at any moment the *Afrika Korps* might crack. The British
commander had succeeded beyond all expectations. Now might
come the moment of triumph.

Instead, for Auchinleck came the moment of personal tragedy.
The day after Rommel wrote this letter Winston Churchill arrived
in Cairo, *en route* for talks in Moscow with Stalin, and the British
Prime Minister planned to relieve Auchinleck of his command.

Lack of clear decision in the desert fighting during July had convinced Churchill of the need for drastic changes; even Brooke failed to realise the extent of Auchinleck's achievement and had become increasingly concerned over the situation – the British army seemed utterly weary, demoralised and 'punch-drunk'. A signal from Auchinleck on 31 July had reinforced Churchill's opinion that another British commander must be chosen for the Middle East. 'Reluctantly concluded,' wired Auchinleck, 'that in present circumstances renewal of our efforts to break enemy front or turn his southern flank not feasible ... Opportunity for resumption of offensive operations unlikely to arise before mid-September.' Auchinleck believed that by September he would be able to reorganise, re-supply and train the 8th Army to the best advantage, having had time to instil his forces with new spirit. He would never have the chance; late on 6 August a signal arrived in London from Churchill in Cairo which led to a special meeting of the War Cabinet early next morning. 'As a result of such inquiries as I have made here, and after prolonged consultations with Field-Marshal Smuts and CIGS, and Minister of State, I have come to the conclusion that a drastic and immediate change is needed in the High Command.'

Churchill proposed that the command should be split into two: a Near East Command comprising Egypt, Palestine and Syria, with its centre in Cairo, and a Middle East Command, comprising Iran and Iraq with its centre in Basra or Baghdad. Auchinleck would be removed from the desert and offered the latter command. Churchill had decided General Harold Alexander should replace Auchinleck in Cairo, while General W. H. E. Gott would take over the 8th Army – at one point in the previous two days Churchill had offered this last appointment to Brooke, but the CIGS had reluctantly refused. Churchill informed the War Cabinet:

> I have no doubt that changes will impart a new and vigorous impulse to the army, and restore confidence in the Command which I regret does not exist at the present time. Here I must emphasise the need of a new start and vehement action to animate the whole of this vast but baffled and somewhat unhinged organisation.

Ministers in London doubted the wisdom of slicing Middle East Command into two, and opposed the appointment for Auchinleck suggested by Churchill; they felt that

> it would be inadvisable for General Auchinleck, after being removed from his present high command, to be appointed to the new Middle East Command. The impression would be conveyed that this separate command had been created in order to let him down lightly. Moreover, he would not have the confidence of his troops.

A telegram containing these objections was sent to Cairo. Churchill refused to alter his proposal and reacted strongly against the idea of Auchinleck being cast aside completely. 'I doubt if the disasters would have occurred in the western desert if General Auchinleck had not been distracted by the divergent considerations of a too widely extended front.' His reply, reaching London on the evening of the 7th, continued:

> I have no hesitation in proposing Auchinleck's appointment ... He has shown high minded qualities of character and resolution ... There is no officer here or in India who has better credentials ... Nor can I advise that General Auchinleck should be ruined and cast aside as unfit to render any further service ...

Ministers considered the matter at a meeting beginning at 11.15 p.m. on the 7th and lasting until the early hours of the 8th. Two more telegrams arrived from Churchill while the War Cabinet was still in session. 'Deeply regret Gott has just been shot down in the air and killed.' The Prime Minister would have to find another commander for the 8th Army, and his second signal revealed his choice. 'CIGS decisively recommends Montgomery for 8th Army. Smuts and I feel this post must be filled at once. Pray send him by special plane at earliest moment.' The Vice-CIGS left the Cabinet Room to issue instructions, and Ministers agreed to a reply to Churchill, in which they gave in to the Prime Minister except for a request that the new Middle East Command should have a different title to avoid confusion with the old. Churchill eventually agreed to change the name: Middle East Command remained at Cairo while the other half became the Persia and Iraq Command.

Auchinleck had taken no part in the discussions and had remained at the battlefront. On 8 August he received a visit from Colonel Ian Jacob, Assistant Military Secretary to the War Cabinet, who carried a letter from the Prime Minister. Auchinleck read the message in silence; Jacob reported: 'He did not move a muscle and remained outwardly calm.' Churchill wrote that on 23 June Auchinleck himself had mentioned in a cable to the CIGS that he might welcome being relieved. 'At that time of crisis for the Army, HMG did not wish to avail themselves of your highminded offer ... The War Cabinet have now decided, for the reasons which you yourself have used, that the moment has come for a change.' The Prime Minister described the new appointment which he now offered to the desert commander. The offer was declined: Auchinleck preferred temporary retirement, and refused to change his mind in a 'bleak and impeccable' interview with Churchill in Cairo next day, 9 August. Not until the following June would 'the

Opposite Lt-Gen, later Field-Marshal, Sir Claude Auchinleck – 'the Auk' – painted by R. G. Eves a few months before he took over command in the desert.

124

R.G. Eve[...]
1940

Auk' accept another command, returning to India following Wavell's appointment as Viceroy.

Meanwhile, also on 9 August, General Alexander arrived to take over in Cairo. Montgomery had been informed of his appointment early the previous morning and he left for the Middle East on the evening of the 10th.

> Since I had few belongings [wrote this austere, little-known General] my preparations for leaving England had been very simple. Everything I possessed had been destroyed by enemy bombing in Portsmouth in January 1941. I was now going to be given the opportunity to get my own back on the Germans.

On the same day as Montgomery stepped into his aircraft, Winston Churchill departed from Cairo for Tehran on the start of his journey to Moscow. The Prime Minister had momentous plans to announce to the Soviet leader, in which Alexander, Montgomery and the 8th Army would play a prominent part. After months of heated arguments between the American and British Chiefs of Staff, and after frequent interventions by President Roosevelt and the Prime Minister, the allies had at last forged a powerful strategic programme. Cross-Channel operations would be launched in 1944; first would come a mighty assault in North Africa from north, east and west. While the re-vitalised 8th Army pushed Rommel back from Egypt, landings would be made far to the west in French North Africa. The latter campaign, 'Torch', would comprise the largest amphibious operation so far in the history of war, and would mark the introduction of American troops into the ground war against Germany. Scheduled target date for 'Torch' was for some time in October – two months away. No time could be lost before the resumption of the offensive by the 8th Army at El Alamein.

General Harold Alexander, courteous, quiet, and renowned for his brilliant fighting withdrawal against the Japanese in Burma, soon displayed his excellent administrative and planning abilities. Alexander and Montgomery had long been close friends; the latter had been a Corps Commander under Alexander at Southern Command in England after Dunkirk, and the two men shared similar views on military tactics. Alexander therefore had confidence in his subordinate, and this allowed him to pursue a remarkably efficient policy in the war against the Axis in the desert:
the Middle East Commander permitted his 8th Army commander

almost complete freedom, and gave him superb support with supplies, encouragement – and protection against interference from London. On 19 August he issued his general brief to Montgomery: preparations must be made to attack the Axis forces with a view to destroying them at the earliest possible moment, and meanwhile the 8th Army must hold its present position.

Montgomery had arrived in Cairo on the 12th, and although he did not officially assume command until the 15th, he immediately immersed himself in hectic activity. 'From what I had learnt the troops had their tails down and there was no confidence in the higher command. This would have to be put right at once.' Within hours of his arrival he flew down to the desert and began making drastic plans for personnel changes, redeployment of forces, the creation of a new armoured force – the 10th Corps – and the injection of new spirit into the troops who would soon be under his command. With the latter, he in fact continued the policy which Auchinleck had already begun, but when Churchill returned to

One of the multitude of men whose individual reports accumulated to provide intelligence assessments of Rommel's intentions. This soldier is positioned far forward, camouflaged with white overalls and his Bren gun well covered.

127

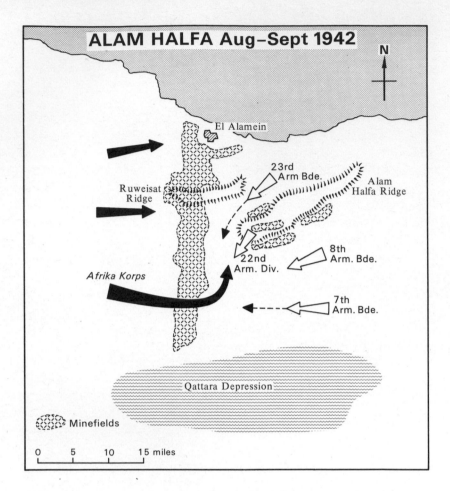

ALAM HALFA Aug–Sept 1942

N

El Alamein

Ruweisat Ridge

23rd Arm Bde.

Alam Halfa Ridge

22nd Arm. Div.

8th Arm. Bde.

Afrika Korps

7th Arm. Bde.

Qattara Depression

Minefields

0   5   10   15 miles

Cairo on the 18th after his visit to Moscow he gave Montgomery, and not his predecessor, the credit for changes which were apparently detectable. 'I am sure we were heading for disaster under the former regime,' reported Churchill to the War Cabinet on the 21st after a trip to see Montgomery in the desert. 'A complete change of atmosphere has taken place.' This signal added: 'It seems probable that Rommel will attack during the moon period before the end of August.'

British Intelligence reports proved accurate. Rommel had decided that the only course open to him was a desperate bid to break through to Cairo and the Canal. To retreat would be politically impossible – Hitler would never agree to such a disgrace – and Rommel's own temperament rebelled against the idea; equally unsavoury was the policy of standing and waiting whilst the British built up their strength, enjoying better supply communications. Yet the Desert Fox knew his attack could only be launched with tremendous difficulties and dangers. Malta still remained unbeaten and the allies threatened Axis convoys across the Mediterranean; Rommel was acutely short of all kinds of resources: his German divisions were about 16,000 under strength, and about 85 per cent of his transport consisted of captured allied vehicles for which spares were extremely limited. Rommel reckoned he was short of 210 tanks, 175 troop-carriers and armoured cars; rations for his men were 'miserable and so monotonous that we were sick of the sight of them', and ammunition stocks had run so low that severe restrictions had to be placed on firing. The RAF had increased its predominance over the *Luftwaffe*. It seemed only a miracle could bring Rommel victory in the forthcoming battle, to be known as Alam Halfa.

Rommel issued orders for the attack to begin on the night of 30 August. He confided in his medical adviser, Forster. 'Professor,' he declared, 'the decision I have taken to attack today is the hardest I have ever taken. Either the army in Russia succeeds in getting through to Grozny and we in Africa manage to reach the Suez Canal, or ...' The Desert Fox shrugged.

Once again Rommel's plan displayed both simplicity and daring. He intended to block in the north, feint against Ruweisat Ridge in the centre and sweep round the British in the south with the *Afrika Korps* – almost a repetition of his offensive against the Gazala Line the previous May. The southern sweep would start to advance during darkness on the 30th, aiming at a penetration of the enemy minefields, after which it would wheel to the north for the main action. The first part presented acute risks: the 15th and 21st Panzer Divisions would have to advance thirty miles in seven hours, at night over unknown terrain and through the British mines. Rommel hoped these mines would be sown less thickly than estimated, and that the British would be preoccupied by the 8th Army changeover of command and by training new units. If his strike to the south could be achieved, he reckoned his infantry could pin the enemy to the Alamein line while the 21st Panzer units raced to outflank Alexandria and while the 15th Panzer and 90th Light forged forward for Cairo.

But Rommel, ill from gastric troubles, nasal diphtheria and poor circulation, utterly weary, his muscles weak, had severely underestimated both the character and preparations of his enemy. Churchill's signal to the War Cabinet on 21 August revealed full awareness of the coming attack, and as early as 27 July Auchinleck's able Deputy Chief of Staff, Major-General E. Dorman-Smith, had submitted an appreciation in which he had predicted   129 that a defensive battle would have to be fought in the Alam Halfa area. Prophetically, he also forecast a later battle in which the British would attempt to smash through the enemy positions about El Alamein. Montgomery later claimed that these plans submitted by Dorman-Smith were never given to him, and he alleged Auchinleck had told him that the 8th Army would fall back if Rommel attacked as was expected. No evidence of any plan by Auchinleck for a withdrawal can be found, and such a retirement policy would have been completely out of line with the 'Auk's' previous principles.

Nevertheless, Montgomery himself now presented a strong contrast to Rommel: 'Monty' was as fresh and vigorous as the Desert Fox was exhausted and stale. He had wasted no time in preparing his defences. He intended to draw the enemy attack into a carefully planned trap. While Australian, South African, Indian, New Zealand and British formations held the line running south from the sea and El Alamein itself, the 22nd Armoured Brigade tanks would be dug in on the well-defended positions between this line and Alam Halfa ridge. Behind these tanks would be the 23rd Armoured Brigade acting as reserve, and to the east would be the 8th Armoured Brigade; further south would be the 7th Armoured Division, then consisting of light formations, which would harry Rommel's flank and rear while the bulk of the *Afrika Korps* ran headlong on to the main British armour to the north.

Nor could Rommel even hope for surprise over the actual timing of the assault. Even before the *Afrika Korps* had begun to breach the minefields on the night of the 30th the RAF were dropping flares and Wellingtons were bombing the Axis units. Motorised infantry of the 7th Armoured harassed the attackers as they struggled through the minefields – unexpectedly thick – and the clear moonlight robbed the enemy of a protective night cloak. The pace of the assault slowed drastically, hence removing Rommel's last possible advantage, speed. By morning on 31 August the Desert Fox had virtually lost the battle, even before British armour had been engaged. Yet Rommel, in his sickness and frustration, gave the fatal order: the attack must be maintained. He only made one change from his original intentions: the *Afrika Korps* would swing north as soon as possible, rather than advancing further to the east before making the turn, in the hope of catching the British off-balance. Even this motivated against the Germans: the earlier change of direction caused the panzers to move more neatly towards the dug-in tanks of the 22nd Armoured Brigade to the west of Alam Halfa ridge. General Sir Brian Horrocks, whom Montgomery had had flown out from England to command the 13th Corps, had held an exercise before the battle to practise dealing with precisely such an offensive, and during this rehearsal markers had been placed along the path of the enemy advance to provide British gunners with exact ranges. As each panzer nosed past the aiming posts they therefore came under devastating fire.

Only one factor worked in Rommel's favour: the weather deteriorated during the 31st and from about 11.30 a.m. dust storms prevented the RAF from striking. Rommel demanded continued advance, despite mounting casualties; by mid-afternoon the *Afrika Korps* had been reorganised and began to roll forward again. Rommel summoned all possible strength, including the few tanks which had recently arrived in the desert for his army, among them Mark IV Specials which had improved armour and a long 75-mm gun able to penetrate at 3,000 yards.

Brigadier Roberts, commanding 22nd Armoured, watched these tanks grind towards his positions.

> On they come, a most impressive array ... It is fascinating to watch them, as one might watch a snake curl up ready to strike. But there is something unusual too ... These Mark IVs have a very long gun on them; in fact it looks like the devil of a gun. This must be the long-barrelled stepped-up 75 mm the Intelligence people have been talking about. And now they all turn left and face us and begin to advance slowly ... I warn all units over the air not to fire until the enemy are within 1,000 yards; it can't be long now ... The battle is on. Once one is in the middle of a battle time is difficult to judge, but it seems only a few minutes before nearly all the tanks of the Grant Squadron of the CLY (County of London Yeomanry) are on fire. The new German 75 mm is taking heavy toll ... The situation is serious; there is a complete hole in our defences.

Roberts sought urgent help from his reserve, the Royal Scots Greys – famous for their cavalry exploits at Waterloo.

> I hurriedly warn the Greys that they must move at all speed from their defensive positions and plug the gap. Meanwhile the enemy tanks are edging forward again and they have got close to the Rifle Brigade's anti-tank guns, who have held their fire marvellously to a few hundred yards. When they open up they inflict heavy casualties on the enemy, but through sheer weight of numbers some guns are overrun. The SOS artillery fire is called for; it comes down almost at once right on top of the enemy's tanks ... But where are the Greys? 'Come on the Greys' I shout over the wireless, 'Get out your whips ...'

The Greys arrived and plunged into the maelstrom; the gap was filled in the fading light; 23rd Armoured Brigade shifted forward in support.

Afrika Korps tanks move forward, passing two burnt-out British lorries.

Rommel had to order his tanks to withdraw. The RAF struck again during the night, and the German commander became increasingly anxious over his fuel situation; yet he threw his forces forward again next day, 1 September, in a futile attempt by 15th Panzer to take the Halfa ridge. Battle continued on the 2nd, but Rommel realised the position was hopeless; retreat began on 3 September. Montgomery made only minimal attempts to hinder the enemy's withdrawal: during the battle he had considered a thrust forward after the Germans had begun to pull back, but soon decided to preserve his army intact for the next, decisive, clash. The only important effort to harass Rommel's retreat came on the 3rd, when New Zealand troops and part of the 132nd Brigade made a night attack – the latter suffered seven hundred casualties, a large proportion of the 8th Army's total losses in the battle. Montgomery came under criticism for allowing the enemy to escape, but he had ample reason for satisfaction. On 7 September the War Cabinet were informed that

> our losses were light ... Rommel had lost about eighty tanks and very large numbers of motor vehicles. We had lost fifty-two tanks, but we had remained in possession of the battlefield and a number of these might be reconditioned. The enemy front was now being held by Italians while the German forces were withdrawn to regroup ...

Tank casualties given to the British Ministers were later proved optimistic: Rommel had lost forty-nine, plus fifty-five field and anti-tank guns and 395 vehicles. Nearly 3,000 Germans and Italians were killed, wounded or captured. The British lost more tanks –

sixty-eight – plus 1,640 men and eighteen anti-tank guns. But more important than the statistics were the intangible benefits of the victory. Montgomery's army had responded well to his leadership; Rommel's forces had once again suffered a heavy blow to morale. Alam Halfa, termed by both British and German authorities as 'a turning point', must be linked to operations conducted by Auchinleck at the Alamein line in early July, when the British commander had wielded his tired forces in such a way that the balance had begun to tilt away from Rommel, and when the RAF had begun to win air supremacy. During Alam Halfa the Desert Air Force had flown 2,500 sorties, and the US Army Air Force had undertaken 180; Rommel had been completely incapable of regaining the initiative. His desert reign was almost done. Now must come the second battle of Alamein.

> My first encounter with Rommel was of great interest [wrote Montgomery to a friend in England just after Alam Halfa]. Luckily I had time to tidy up the mess and to get my plans laid, so there was no difficulty in seeing him off. I feel that I have won the first game, when it was his service. Next time it will be my service, the score being one-love.

The confident 8th Army commander continued his preparations. These would accelerate during September and October, with further personnel changes, regrouping, building elaborate devices to deceive the enemy, and session after session of training and rehearsal. Montgomery took care to introduce himself to his men, visiting as many units as possible.

> The Great Man arrives punctually [wrote Private Crimp in his diary on 20 September]. His name's Montgomery, and he's only recently reached the Middle East, having been specially sent out from Blighty to shake things up … He's supposed to be visiting all the 8th Army units in turn, to size them up and instil a little pep. He proves to be a quiet, severe sort of chap, smallish but tough, with short moustache, pointed features, broody, aggressive grey eyes and a wound-scar on the back of his neck. The inspection lasts a long while, but the General, accompanied by the usual retinue of brass hats, holds it in a steady grip, moving slowly along the ranks, methodically scrutinizing each man – up from the boots, then shooting a quizzical glance at the face with sudden upward lunge of his head.

Alexander and Montgomery received the familiar pressure from London for the offensive to be launched in minimum time. Much depended on North Africa – even the Prime Minister's political position. The public at home urgently needed a decisive victory. 'There may be trouble ahead,' Brendan Bracken, Minister of Information, warned Churchill's physician. 'The Prime Minister

Gunners await the next battle. Sketched by E. Ardizzoni.

must win his battle in the desert or get out ... There is a good deal going on under the surface.' Churchill became increasingly fretful and emotional. Quarrels had arisen between the allies over plans for the landings in French North Africa, operation 'Torch', and the target date for the amphibious attack had been put back to 8 November. After days of anxious debate it was finally agreed at the start of September that American troops would land at Casablanca, despite British fears over difficulties which the GIs would encounter with the Atlantic swell; more would land at Oran, and others at Algiers with British troops following an hour later.

But for political and military reasons, 'Torch' must be preceded by a British offensive against Rommel in the east. 'I am anxiously awaiting some account of your intentions,' cabled Churchill to Alexander on the 17th. Two days later the General replied that Montgomery would launch his Alamein offensive on 24 October – operation 'Lightfoot'. Churchill sought an earlier date, but Alexander signalled on the 21st: 'If I were to be obliged to carry out this operation before my target date, I should not only be not satisfied with the chance of success, but I should be definitely apprehensive as to the result.' Montgomery later wrote: 'I had told Alexander privately that ... if a September attack was ordered by Whitehall,

134

they would have to get someone else to do it.' Brooke had a 'hammer and tongs' argument with the Prime Minister on the 23rd, but later in the day Churchill cabled to Alexander: 'We are in your hands, and of course a victorious battle makes amends for much delay.' Ironically, the offensive would be launched far after the date which Auchinleck had previously contemplated – and yet Auchinleck's inability to find an earlier target had been among the main reasons for his dismissal. Also on Wednesday, 23 September, Rommel left the desert for home, under doctor's orders. 'Mussolini is convinced that Rommel will not come back,' wrote the Italian Foreign Minister, Ciano, in his diary on the 27th. 'He finds Rommel physically and morally shaken.'

The days fled by. 'Training is strenuous,' wrote Private Crimp on 8 October, 'and there are many portents of approaching action. All the other camps in the area are now filled with infantry, tank and artillery units.' Crimp also commented: 'Most people feel, to put it mildly, a bit doubtful about the latest GOC. They don't like his "new-broom" policy and consider his methods extreme.' But in London the War Cabinet heard an optimistic report from General Smuts on 14 October, after the South African leader had visited Egypt. 'The change in the 8th Army ... was unbelievable. Our tank position was very strong. The training of the troops had been well carried out. We could look forward to the results of the battle with some confidence.' Yet Smuts had 'sounded a note of

Training in the desert: long hours were spent perfecting the siting, limbering and loading of guns.

135

Newly-arrived British
troops file into trenches
– part of the prepara-
tions for the battle of
Alamein.

warning' to Alexander – and one which Churchill would have
done well to remember in a few days' time. 'On this occasion there
was no chance of outflanking the enemy. As we were attacking on
so narrow a front, only thirty miles, we would almost certainly
have to fight our way through heavily defended positions.' Smuts
had therefore cautioned Alexander that

> he must be prepared not to meet with immediate success. I had strongly
> advised him, however, to keep on attacking the enemy and to fight his
> way through. We might have to sustain heavy casualties ... But our
> losses were unlikely to be greater than the heavy losses which we had
> suffered in recent retreats. We might have to keep up the pressure of the
> attack for a week.

Alexander had agreed. Smuts added – with words which would
also prove prophetic – that it was important to 'bring the enemy
to book in the area in which the battle took place. It would not be
to our advantage if we had to carry on a battle against a retreating
enemy. We are not very well found in transport.'

Montgomery had issued his 'General Plan' for operation 'Lightfoot' exactly one month earlier, on 14 September. Broadly, the plan

envisaged a push by the infantry of 30th Corps in the north, aimed at breaching the enemy's defences with the help of massive artillery support. The bulk of the armour of 10th Corps would pass through two resulting corridors and position itself 'on ground of its own choosing astride the enemy supply lines'. This would force the enemy tanks to attack, and the more powerful British armour would emerge victorious. Once the panzers had been destroyed, enemy infantry could be rounded up. Further south a secondary attack would be launched by 13th Corps, aimed at preventing the enemy from moving troops to reinforce the northern sector.

During the second half of September the 8th Army GOC began to have doubts; he feared he might be asking too much of his 'somewhat untrained' troops, and in the first week of October he decided to alter the design of the northern plan. Under the new scheme the infantry would still break two corridors through the enemy defences, but these units would then be engaged in widening the gaps, thus methodically destroying the enemy's holding troops. Montgomery called this process 'crumbling'. Enemy tanks would attempt to stop the infantry, but the British armour – having followed the infantry units through the breaches – should be in an excellent position to intervene. The enemy would therefore be given no respite throughout the whole procedure. Montgomery declared:

> Having thus 'eaten the guts' out of the enemy he will have no troops with which to hold a front. His Panzer Army may attempt to interfere with our tactics, and may launch counter-attacks; this would be what we want, and would give us the opportunity of inflicting casualties on the enemy's armour. When we have succeeded in destroying the enemy's holding troops, the eventual fate of the Panzer Army is certain – it will not be able to avoid destruction.

Montgomery therefore relied on sheer weight of numbers, and indeed his numerical superiority over the enemy had grown to impressive proportions. No previous British commander in the desert had enjoyed such a degree of advantage. Tanks had been flowing to the Middle East, among them the 300 Shermans promised by Roosevelt to Churchill on that grim day in June when Tobruk had fallen. These newcomers had a number of innovations, including the 75-mm gun mounted in the turret with all-round traverse. Another new arrival was the British Crusader Mark III, which mounted a six-pounder gun. The 8th Army would have just over 1,000 tanks ready for action, with 200 available as replacement, while about another 1,000 were in workshops. Rommel had about 250 German tanks fit for battle, including thirty-one panzer 137

Field-Marshal the Viscount Alexander of Tunis, by John Leigh-Pemberton, after an original by Sir Oswald Birley.

Mark IIs which were too light to count in combat, plus twenty-three under repair; these were divided almost equally between the 15th and 21st Panzer divisions. Italian tanks numbered 278 medium and twenty light.

The disparity in Axis–British artillery strengths proved even more dramatic than with armour: nearly 1,000 medium and field pieces were available to the 8th Army on the eve of battle, including the new American 105-mm self-propelled gun. Rommel had about half the British total, the vast majority far less powerful. And Montgomery would be able to enjoy the most prized advantage of all – massive air superiority. The Desert Air Force, in direct support of the army, would number about 750 aircraft, 530 of which were serviceable, apart from fifty-four transports, while the Axis air forces in North Africa comprised 275 German aircraft, 150 serviceable, including eighty dive-bombers but no bombers, and 400 Italian aircraft, 200 of which were serviceable – about 350 combat-worthy aircraft in all.

Churchill signalled Alexander on 20 October: '"Torch" goes forward steadily and punctually. But all our hopes are centred upon the battle you and Montgomery are going to fight. It may well be the key to the future.' On the same day Montgomery gave his final address to senior officers. He outlined the main features of the plan and the advantages enjoyed by the British; according to his outline notes for the speech:

> Methodical progress; destroy enemy part by part, slowly and surely. Shoot tanks and shoot Germans. He cannot last a long battle; we can. We must therefore keep at it hard; no unit commander must relax the pressure; organise ahead for a 'dog-fight' of a week. Whole affair about ten days – Don't expect spectacular results too soon.

When he came to speak the words, Montgomery changed his estimate for the length of the battle from ten days to twelve.

The first transports for the 'Torch' landings in French North Africa slipped down the dark Clyde on Thursday, 22 October. In the desert, Montgomery issued a personal message to his men.

> We are ready NOW. The battle which is now about to begin will be one of the decisive battles of history. It will be the turning point of the war. The eyes of the whole world will be on us, watching anxiously which way the battle will swing ...

Churchill had asked Alexander to send him a code signal when the offensive opened; late on Friday, 23 October, this message arrived: 'ZIP'. At 9.40 p.m. massed British guns opened a tremendous barrage on the enemy positions at El Alamein and thousands of infantrymen prepared to surge forward. Rommel remained in Austria; Montgomery asleep in his caravan. 'There was nothing I could do and I knew I would be needed later.'

Chapter 6

El Alamein

Right on time the barrage bursts [wrote Private Crimp]. The whole line leaps into life ... The guns nearby crash incessantly, one against another, searing the darkness with gashes of flame, and those farther up and down the line rumble wrathfully and convulse the northern and southern horizons with ceaseless flashing and flickering. Groups of Jock infantry, in shorts and shirts and tin-hats, with bayonets fixed, begin filtering forward through the gap. Poor devils – I don't envy them their night's work.

For seven thundering minutes the enemy's forward defences received a vicious battering from the full weight of 30th Corps artillery. At zero hour plus seven the fire support began to shift from locality to locality to supply the needs of respective attacking formations, and this pattern would continue for five and a half hours with tremendous strain on both gunners and guns. At 10 p.m. the infantry assaults began, skein after skein of men advancing towards the enemy minefields in the light of the ghastly explosions and beneath the full moon. 'I look straight up into the face of the moon,' commented Crimp, 'which is waxen and pallid and wears an expression, so it seems to me, of incredulous dismay at the fantastic scene being enacted down here on this patch of earth.' Within minutes a haze had drifted up from the dust created by explosives, vehicles and tanks, and this hung heavy over the battlefield, restricting visibility. The pall would remain for almost two terrible weeks.

The four divisions of 30th Corps attacked in line, each on a two-brigade front. Within thirty minutes of the infantry advance the whole six-mile battle frontage had become a writhing mass of men and machines. The battle represented the peculiar evolution of war planning: desperate decisions had been taken weeks or months before by a mere handful of men – Churchill, Brooke, Alexander – and these decisions had affected the lives of millions. Their choice of action had been passed on for thousands of men and women to put into effect, with a myriad of details to be settled. The whole vast machine for military planning had begun to function. And now the process had turned full circle and had reached the end of its cycle. The battle, conceived by so few men, organised and arranged by so many, had begun – and almost immediately became fragmented into hundreds of separate, lonely struggles, as individual and personal as the deliberations of the original small group of men who had begun the process which led to Alamein.

The line had broken up into blobs of men all struggling together [wrote Major H. P. Samwell of the Argylls]. I saw some men in a trench

Opposite 'The tanks came plunging through – hundreds of tanks, .. lunging to the west through the gap ...'

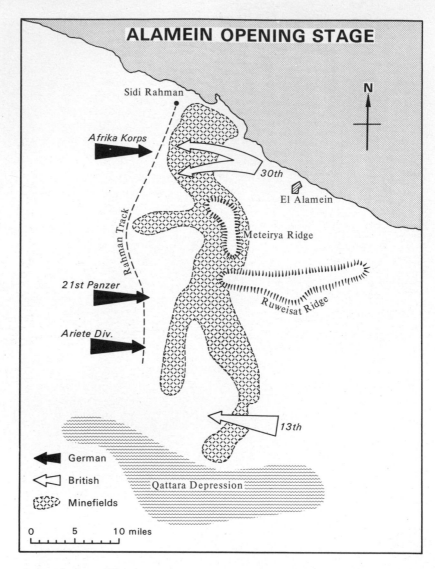

ALAMEIN OPENING STAGE

N

Sidi Rahman

Afrika Korps

30th

El Alamein

Rahman Track

Meteirya Ridge

21st Panzer

Ruweisat Ridge

Ariete Div.

13th

German

British

Minefields

Qattara Depression

0   5   10 miles

ahead of me. They were standing up with their hands above their heads
screaming something that sounded like 'Mardray'. I remember think-
ing how dirty and ill-fitting their uniforms were, and smiled at myself
for bothering about that at this time ... Suddenly I heard a shout of
'Watch out!' and the next moment something hard hit the toe of my
boot and bounced off. There was a blinding explosion ... I was unhurt.
I looked for the sergeant who had been beside me; he had come up to
take the place of the one who had fallen ... I saw him lying sprawled
out on his back groaning. His leg was just a tangled mess ... I suddenly
felt furious; an absolute uncontrollable temper surged up inside me.
I swore and cursed at the enemy now crouching in the corner of the
trench; then I fired at them at point-blank range – one, two, three, and
then clock! I had forgotten to reload. I flung my pistol away in disgust

142

and grabbed a rifle – the sergeant's I think – and rushed in ... I bayoneted two more and then came out again ... I started to wonder what my wife was doing at that moment ...

Small actions such as this experienced by Major Samwell were multiplied a thousand times, and the British infantry swept over the first line of German and Italian defences. But stiffer opposition lay ahead.

Churchill paced his study at Ten Downing Street, snatching at each report from Cairo. So much depended upon those individual blobs of men in the billowing desert, groping through the enemy minefields. By midnight the advance had begun to slow. Enemy defences were stronger, the attacking waves had inevitably become tattered, and the Axis defenders were recovering from the initial artillery bombardment. Very early in the morning, 24 October, anxious messages accumulated at the 8th Army HQ. To the far north Australian, New Zealand, Highland and South African troops had almost reached their planned objectives, but further south another Australian Brigade, two from the Highland Division and one South African had failed to make sufficient headway. Still further south the secondary attack by the 13th Corps had also fallen behind schedule. By dawn the spearhead had been blunted, and British armour which had been crammed in the half-finished mine-field gaps behind the infantry had suffered heavy casualties. Units in the rear anxiously awaited orders to move forward.

'It's first light, eerily quiet,' wrote Crimp, still in the main British defences behind the battle-front. 'There's a reek of cordite, stale and damp.' An armoured break-through had yet to be achieved; Montgomery insisted that the 30th Corps infantry must continue their bloody grind forward against the enemy trenches in the north. He therefore ordered that the two northern corridors must be properly cleared, regardless of cost; the New Zealand Division under Freyberg must start the crumbling process by striking south-wards from the Meteirya Ridge while the 10th Armoured Division passed through this lower gap in the northern sector. The 1st Armoured Division would continue to batter through the northern-most breach. But German and Italian infantrymen clung to their holes and the *Luftwaffe* pounded the massed British armour. The *Afrika Korps* remained intact, despite the loss of the German commander, Stumme, who had suffered a heart attack. Hitler had telephoned Rommel in the Austrian mountains, and the Desert Fox had obeyed the order to return to the desert. 'I knew there were no more laurels to be earned,' he commented. He had 'but small hope of success'.

And as Rommel's light aircraft flew down over Italy late on the 24th, the armoured brigade of 1st Armoured Division wrenched a hole through the upper corridor in the north; tanks began to filter through the gap. Private Crimp saw this armour moving forward.

> New Sherman tanks, in seemingly never-ending numbers, make a heartening sight. A regiment is going by in single file as I scribble this on the back of a message-form pad. Each tank has its name on the side, below the turret: Ajax, Audacious, Attila, Argonaut ... and so on, lurching and grinding and making a terrific din.

Enemy units from the 15th Panzer Division moved to attack this British break-through. 'Exactly what I wanted,' commented Montgomery. Further south the New Zealand Division prepared for another attempt at a 'crumbling' operation while the Desert Air Force continued to strike at enemy defences: during the day the RAF flew about 1,000 sorties.

But now came, in Montgomery's words, 'the real crisis'. Freyberg, commander of the New Zealanders, believed that 10th Armoured, which would support his attack, was not 'properly set up' in the southern corridor. Minefields were deeper than had been expected on Meteirya Ridge, and enemy aircraft had caused heavy damage to the packed British tanks. As night fell on the 24th the flames from these burning wrecks provided excellent guides for further enemy air strikes. Fears for the proposed attack were passed to General Sir Francis de Guingand, Montgomery's Chief of Staff, who decided early on the 25th that the corps commanders must be summoned for a conference, and that Montgomery must be roused from his bed. At 3 a.m. an urgent discussion took place between Montgomery and Generals Leese and Lumsden, respective commanders of the 10th and 30th Corps. Lumsden reported that one of the 10th Armoured regiments, the Staffordshire Yeomanry, had broken through the lower gap in the northern sector, but fears were being felt for these tanks – which would be exposed to concentrated enemy fire when dawn broke. Lumsden said that General Gatehouse, commander of the 10th Armoured, wished to pull back to the relative safety behind the eastern slope of Meteirya Ridge.

Montgomery refused to consider such a plan: he told Lumsden that the original orders must be followed; Lumsden asked Montgomery to speak to Gatehouse on the field telephone. 'I did so at once,' wrote Montgomery in his memoirs, 'and discovered to my horror that he himself was some sixteen thousand yards (nearly ten miles) behind his leading armoured brigades. I spoke to him in no uncertain voice, and ordered him to go forward at once and take charge of his battle: he was to fight his way out, and lead his division from in front and not from behind.' Montgomery kept Lumsden back when the others had left the conference.

> I said I was determined that the armoured divisions would get out of the minefield area and into the open where they could manoeuvre; any wavering or lack of firmness now would be fatal. If he himself, or the commander 10th Armoured Division, was not 'for it', then I would appoint others who were.

The battle hung in the balance during the night of the 24th/25th. Far to the south the subsidiary attack by the 13th Corps had failed to make ground. At 11.30 a.m. on the 25th Montgomery met Alexander and then conferred again with his two corps commanders. More tanks from 10th Armoured had managed to force through the lower corridor in the northern sector, but at 7 a.m. they had been obliged to retire to the cover of the ridge – as Gatehouse had feared. The 1st Armoured Division, which had pierced the top corridor the previous day, had made no further headway against enemy anti-tank defences, and had lost about twenty-four machines. Montgomery now decided he must change his plans, despite his obstinate stand with his subordinates the previous night. Attempts by the New Zealand Division to strike south from the lower corridor would be too costly; instead the 30th Corps units in this area would continue to hold Meteirya Ridge. From the upper corridor would come a strike north towards the coast using 145 the 9th Australian Division, and the 10th Corps was to press west and north-west from the positions gained in this upper breach.

> It is clear [signalled Alexander to Brooke during the evening of the 25th] that the enemy intends to fight in his forward positions and that the struggle for mastery will be fierce and probably prolonged over a considerable period, so that for about a week it will not be possible to give reliable appreciations of how events will develop. The first phase of the battle – the break-in – opened and proceeded much according to plan ... The second phase – the debouchment of armour west of minefields – did not progress as rapidly as was hoped, but by this morning it had been completed and operations following on from that are now in progress but are not yet clearly defined.

Alexander's report proved more optimistic than the facts warranted and clearly reflected the permanent confidence felt by Montgomery. War Cabinet Ministers meeting on the 26th therefore received a somewhat unbalanced picture: 'In the extreme north enemy counter attack was repelled, and our own troops mopped up isolated enemy resistance in their final objective. The passage of our armoured formations through the gaps in the enemy minefield was delayed ... but eventually it was completed.' News had still to reach London of the attempt by the Australians to push north from the upper corridor the previous night, 25/26 October: this operation gained ground and brought the Australians closer to the coast road, but the attackers suffered heavy losses. And now Rommel had returned to the fight.

Fierce fighting continued throughout the 26th and 27th. Men collapsed from heat and exhaustion; wounded lay with flies covering their faces; Rommel wrote: 'Rivers of blood were poured out over miserable strips of land which, in normal times, not even the poorest Arab would have bothered his head about.' Scraps of featureless territory such as Kidney Ridge – which amounted to no more than an undulation in the ground – achieved monumental significance. The Desert Fox watched his armour suffering increasing casualties against the superior British artillery and aircraft, and became anxious over his fuel supplies for his remaining tanks. 'I reported to the Führer's HQ that we would lose the battle unless there was an immediate improvement in the supply situation. Judging by previous experience, there was little hope of this happening.' But Montgomery also felt rising apprehension. Between 23 and 26 October about 300 British tanks were put out of action, and his infantry formations were becoming weaker.

On the 26th he decided to limit the main offensive to another push northwards by the Australians; a substantial reserve would be created, by re-grouping, for another major blow. By 28 October,

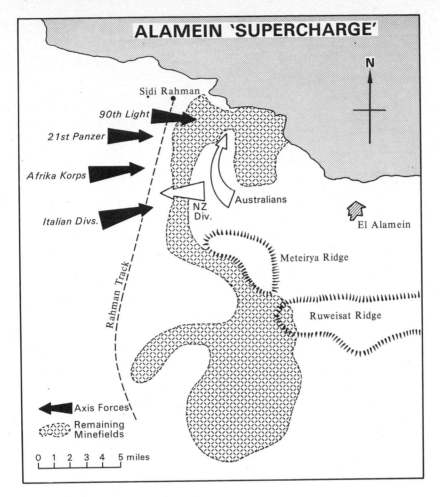

ALAMEIN 'SUPERCHARGE'

N

Sidi Rahman

90th Light

21st Panzer

Afrika Korps

Italian Divs.

Rahman Track

NZ Div.

Australians

El Alamein

Meteirya Ridge

Ruweisat Ridge

← Axis Forces

Remaining Minefields

0 1 2 3 4 5 miles

after further heavy fighting, his fears had multiplied. 'I began to realise from the casualty figures that I must be careful. I knew the final blow must be put in on 30th Corps' front (the northern sector), but at the moment I was not clear exactly where. But I had to get ready for it.' He therefore decided to turn the southern flank, the bogged 13th Corps, entirely over to the defensive, thus allowing more divisions to be placed in reserve. Some armoured formations in the north were also pulled back. These would be used for the massive attempt to break through the German final defences, operation 'Supercharge', intended to begin on the 31st.

Montgomery planned to launch this attack as far north as possible, in the area where the Australians were operating, but on 29 October intelligence reports indicated that Rommel had now committed his best armour in this sector, including the 90th Light, with the obvious aim of blocking the very move which Montgomery intended. The Desert Fox had anticipated his enemy's plans – but had done so too soon. 'This means a change,' commented Montgomery, and he now proceeded to alter the direction of 'Supercharge': the Australians should make a third attempt to strike towards the sea on the night of the 30th to keep Rommel committed, but the main attack would come further south just above the lower corridor. By shifting northwards, Rommel had separated his German formations from the Italian: Montgomery would strike at the hinge of the two enemy armies, with the greatest weight falling on the Italians. All the British commander's cockiness had returned as he ordered preparations for the final blow.

In London, suspense had reached snapping-point. Despite the warning from Smuts that the pressure might have to be exerted for a week, and despite Alexander's signal of the 25th saying it might take this long before an appreciation could be sent, Churchill could stand the wait no longer. When news reached London of Montgomery's redeployment and withdrawal of certain units – with the information not backed by any details of 'Supercharge' – the Prime Minister exploded with anger. Violent arguments took place between Churchill and Brooke during the morning of the 29th, after which Ministers were summoned for an urgent meeting of the Defence Committee. Brooke soothed the Prime Minister as much as possible, but a cable sent to Cairo after this session nevertheless contained implied criticism. 'The Defence Committee feel that the general situation justifies all the risks and sacrifices involved in the relentless prosecution of this battle.' Brooke was himself suffering doubts – 'these had to be kept entirely to myself.' In response to appeals for enlightenment, Montgomery's Chief of Staff merely told Casey, Minister of State in Cairo, 'to tell Whitehall not to bellyache.'

The Australians launched their attack on the night of the 30th, as planned, and gained positions across the coastal road and railway after courageous fighting. 'Supercharge', due to be started the following night, had to be delayed for another twenty-four hours while the complicated redeployment could be completed. Meanwhile the infantry had continued to press the Axis defenders and to withstand counter-attacks.

For the next half-hour we get a concentrated dose [jotted Crimp in his tattered diary during one action]. It's most unpleasant crouching in the bottom of the pit, packed tight with even more chaps ... The shells scream down in inexorable succession, and all around us is the driving, rending crash of high explosive. Several times my tin-hat is crushed on to my head by the impact of nearby detonations, and once my lungs

are filled by a rush of sand. Everyone lies still. You can't do a thing – it just has to happen.

At 1 a.m. on Monday, 2 November, the tanks and infantry advanced again for operation 'Supercharge', attacking on a front of four thousand yards to a depth of six thousand yards, and aimed at wrenching apart the German and Italian formations. Within minutes this sector of the front had become an inferno –

the brittle rasping and spitting of machine-guns; mortar-bombs keeling over, whispering gently, and crashing suddenly; solids blasting like express trains, leaving groaning, feverish turmoils of vacuum in their wake; and the mewing and squealing chorus of 25-pounder shells ...

Infantry units managed to reach their objectives just to the north of the lower corridor and forced a gap for the British armour surging

Tobruk burns while British troops and tanks wait to enter the town; the armour displays the famous Desert Rat insignia.

149

Armoured cars leap
through a gap in the
enemy minefields to
wheel round behind the
enemy, and to batter an
opening for the 8th
Army tanks.

behind them. Crimp overheard a typical conversation on a tank squadron's short-range wireless network:

'Hallo, 11. Can you find out what's going on in front of you?'
'Sorry Angus. Can't see a damn thing ...'
'Hullo 15. Just tell George to move over to his right a bit. I don't seem to get him from here ...'
'Fraid I don't get him either Angus. His set must be u/s.'
'Hallo 8. There's something over on my left. I can't quite make out what. Looks like a row of funny little squat, square things.'

Crimp continued:

Suddenly there's a colossal WHOOSH-BANG, and a sheet of flame leaps across the darkness ahead. Then another tremendous crash, and a tank in front seems to disintegrate in a searing flash of light. My heart freezes. Those 'funny little squat, square things' are obviously Jerry anti-tank guns ... The tanks seem hesitant, uncertain what to do in the darkness. A voice bellows urgently over the inter-comm ... 'For Christ's sake, get spread out!'

Hardest task of all had been given to the 9th Armoured Brigade, which had to exploit the infantry success by pushing on towards the Sidi Rahman track and hold the door open for the 1st Armoured Division. John Currie, commanding the 9th, had warned that his men would suffer terrible losses in this advance against a wall of guns, but Montgomery had declared: 'It's got to be done, and, if necessary, I am prepared to accept 100 per cent casualties.' The Brigade now lost seventy out of its ninety-four tanks, although many were later recovered, and 230 officers and men were killed and wounded. But thirty-five enemy guns were destroyed and the brigade held on long enough for two brigades of the 1st Armoured Division to screech out of the minefield corridor and deploy.

The battle had still to be won – by the end of the 3rd the 1st Armoured had been reduced by fourteen tanks destroyed and forty damaged or broken down – but sheer strength and persistence had begun to tell. The *Afrika Korps* was bleeding to death; on the morning of the 2nd the panzer commander, von Thomas, had reported to Rommel that 'the front was holding, but only just', and the Desert Fox decided late on the 2nd that he must start to pull back. 'I hoped to be able to salvage at least part of the infantry.' Then, at 1.30 a.m. on the 3rd, Rommel received a chilling message from Hitler. 'There can be no other thought but to stand fast, yield not a yard of room and throw every gun and every man into the battle.' The German commander sent an *aide* to Hitler to plead for a reversal of this no-retreat policy; meanwhile the Führer's order had thrown him into despair. 'A kind of apathy took hold of us as we issued orders for all existing positions to be held.' Indian and Highland troops punched hard again during the night of the 3rd; the Axis line cracked still further; the *Afrika Korps* had now been reduced to a mere thirty tanks. Hitler relented, and before dawn on Wednesday, 4 November, Rommel ordered the retreat – fully expecting to be encircled and annihilated in the process.

Churchill wept as he read a signal from Alexander: 'After twelve days of heavy and violent fighting the 8th Army has inflicted a severe defeat on the German and Italian forces under Rommel's command ...' The historian of the 4th Indian Division described the moment of triumph:

> The guns lifted and were done; there was quiet but for the crackle of small-arms fire. Out in front little figures scuttled madly, seeking holes. A carrier platoon went out to bring them in. Then another noise, thunder out of the east, and more thunder. The roar mounted. The tanks came plunging through – hundreds of tanks, lunging to the west through the gap the Wedge had made, and wheeling north for the kill. The sun rose on the last of Alamein.

Rommel escaped. The remnants of his army fled back from the havoc of battle, and the 8th Army proved unable to turn victory into crushing destruction of the Axis forces. Montgomery, for all his confidence before and during the battle, had made insufficient plans to reap the rewards of the expected result. No forces had been created for a vigorous pursuit; all had been committed in the fighting, and the 8th Army had long lacked adequate transport vehicles – as Smuts had warned the War Cabinet prior to the opening of battle. Now the enemy could only be pursued by the formations which had been in the thick of the front-line fight, and these, including the mobile New Zealand infantry brigades and the 1st, 7th, 8th and 9th Armoured, were too scattered, too exhausted, or too involved with enemy rearguard positions, to be able to begin an aggressive pursuit in time. 'The pursuit proper,' wrote Montgomery in his memoirs, 'began on the 5th November.' But by then almost twenty-four hours had passed since the enemy had begun to pull back; early on the 5th Rommel had set up a temporary HQ at Fuka and during the day *Afrika Korps* units had reached this point, including 90th Light. By 6 November some German units were reaching Sollum, despite continuous RAF attacks and congested roads which Rommel termed 'indescribable'.

Then, during the evening of the 6th, torrents of rain began to fall and these would continue for the next twenty-four hours. Montgomery claimed that 'only the rain … saved them from complete annihilation', but this ignored the fact that the downpours which hindered his pursuit also affected the German retreat. The main advantage brought by the bad weather was the restriction of RAF strikes, but these alone could not have destroyed the fleeing *Afrika Korps*. Yet Alamein remained a tremendous victory, both in terms of material and morale. Montgomery's 8th Army suffered 13,560 men killed, wounded and missing; nearly 500 tanks had been put out of action, although most could be repaired; 111 guns of various kinds had been lost. The RAF had suffered seventy-seven aircraft casualties, and the Americans twenty. The *Luftwaffe* lost fewer aircraft – sixty-four – and the Italians only twenty, but these totals must be compared with the numbers of sorties flown – nearly 10,500 for the RAF, 1,181 for the Americans – and only 1,550 for the *Luftwaffe* and an estimated 1,570 Italian. The British had taken an enormous battering, indicative of the terrible slogging match. But German losses were frightful. On 4 November Rommel had only about thirty-six tanks left out of 249, and the Italians had about half their total of 278, most of which would be lost in the first hours of retreat in an encounter with the 7th Armoured Division. By 7 November three-quarters of the Axis guns had either been captured or destroyed and the number of prisoners had topped 20,000.

And on 8 November the enemy in North Africa received another punishing blow, this time through a stab in the back. Allied naval columns zigzagged towards the shore at Algiers, Oran and Casablanca; convoy ships spawned scores of smaller craft, and the waves of 'Torch' crashed against the beaches far behind Rommel's retreating army. Three mighty Task Forces were being employed. In the west, 35,000 American troops under Major-General George S. Patton had sailed direct from America to brave the Atlantic swell at Casablanca; the centre force of 39,000 American troops, sailing from Britain under Major-General L. R. Fredendall, had been aimed at Oran; the eastern task force would deal with Algiers, spearheaded by an Anglo-American assault and followed by the first elements of the British 1st Army under General K. A. N. Anderson. The three prongs would strike for Tunis under the overall command of General Dwight D. Eisenhower, now at his Gibraltar HQ. The drive east to Tunis, combined with the 8th Army's pursuit of Rommel in the west, would catch the Germans and Italians in a relentless allied vice. The whole balance of the war, so long weighted in Axis favour, would alter. As Churchill declared

at a meeting in the City of London: 'This is not the end. It is not even the beginning of the end. But it is, perhaps, the end of the beginning.' The Prime Minister had once again become buoyant; Rommel immediately realised the implications of 'Torch'. 'This spelt the end of the army in Africa,' he declared.

But one paramount problem faced the American and British troops landing at Casablanca, Oran and Algiers. American hopes had been high that the French would co-operate in this invasion of their colonial Moroccan and Algerian territory, hence the US insistence that GIs should provide the major contingents rather than the British who were most disliked by the Vichy French Government. But on Sunday, 8 November, these hopes faded. Frenchmen took up arms against the allies at Algiers, Oran and in the Casablanca area; the unwelcome hostilities could impose a disastrous delay on the allied advance, giving the Germans and Italians more time to build up forces for the fight for Tunis: the 560 mountainous miles between Algiers and Tunis had to be travelled in minimum time to prevent the Axis from regaining the

The opening of the Allied North African Headquarters, November 1942. Left to right: Lt-Gen Clark, Admiral Cunningham, Lt-Gen Anderson and Admiral Darlan.

155

initiative. At Algiers, the most important target for the 'Torch' landings, resistance ended at 7 p.m. on the 8th, but fighting continued elsewhere.

The situation became further complicated when the allies discovered the arrival in Algiers of Admiral J. F. Darlan, C-in-C of all French forces, pro-Vichy and anti-British, and a firm believer that France's best chance lay in co-operation with the Germans unless the Americans could prove themselves the stronger. Delicate negotiations to secure French help in the diplomatic and military fields threatened to founder with the presence of this aged but powerful figure. The Americans sent General Henri Giraud into North Africa as a potential pro-allied French leader, but he immediately found himself eclipsed by the far more influential Darlan; Eisenhower encouraged talks between General Giraud and Admiral Darlan, and on 11 November the two Frenchmen came to terms: the Admiral confirmed the General as C-in-C French forces in North Africa, in return for Giraud's recognition of Darlan as the supreme civil authority. The agreement, endorsed by Eisenhower, would create storms of anger in Britain, smacking as it did of approval for Darlan's collaboration with the Germans and threatening to oust Britain's own prickly favourite for French leadership, General Charles de Gaulle. But as Brooke told the War Cabinet on 21 November: 'In the present military situation we ought not to take any risks. We were dependent on French support for communication ... Time was of the essence in the matter, as it was important to avoid giving the enemy any opportunity to establish himself strongly in Tunisia.' Oran had surrendered at noon on 10 November, and the tragic fighting between French patriots and the Americans had ended. The allies could now move east.

The initial advance into Tunisia was to be made mainly by British troops, and General Anderson had kept the 36th Infantry Brigade Group tactically loaded afloat for a further landing at Bougie, 120 miles east of Algiers and 300 miles west of Tunis. This move was successfully undertaken on the 11th, but the enemy reacted swiftly with the *Luftwaffe* sinking four ships before RAF fighters could give protection. 'Events moving fast,' wrote Brooke in his diary. Next day, 12 November, two companies of the 3rd Parachute Battalion dropped onto Bône airfield, even closer to the Tunisian border, arriving just ahead of a German parachute unit which had to return frustrated to base. Later the same day 6th Commando came ashore at Bône, and Spitfires clattered in to start operating from the airfield. Also on the 12th, 8th Army units once

Medenine. German
tanks advance against
well-prepared Scots
Guards positions on
6 March. 'The
rumbling they made
was terrific and it
gradually got nearer,'
wrote the Scots Guards
historian. Painted by
Terence Cuneo.

more arrived at Tobruk. Mussolini had pressed Rommel to make a stand at Sollum, but the Desert Fox had realised the futility: of the thirty tanks which 21st Panzer had rescued from Alamein, only four were now intact. Fresh pleas were made to Rommel for a defence at El Agheila on the Cyrenaica–Tripolitania border, but all available German reinforcements were being diverted from Rommel for the Axis defence of Tunisia in the face of advancing 'Torch' troops. Tunisia had never been envisaged as a theatre of war by the Germans or Italians; now all efforts were being made for the imminent battle. Aircraft had begun to arrive on the day after the 'Torch' landings, and their numbers were increasing; on 12 November General Nehring, former *Afrika Korps* commander, was entrusted with the defence of the country, and by the 14th German paratroopers were occupying the city of Tunis and its harbour. Two days later parachutists had their first clash with British units from 'Torch': these, from the 78th Division, had been ordered to advance on Bizerta. The Battle of Tunisia had begun.

Also on 16 November, members of the War Cabinet in London heard latest details of the situation in both the 'Torch' and 8th Army area. With the former, 'German strength in Tunisia might now be about 6,000 to 8,000. Reinforcements were continually arriving. Our forces had just crossed into Tunisia from Algeria …' On the other North African front, 'our forces in Libya had reached Martuba … the pursuit of the defeated enemy continued'. Next day men from the 1st Parachute Division were successfully dropped at Souk el Arba, twenty miles over the Tunisian border in the west, where they commandeered buses and were forty miles forward at Beja by nightfall; early the following morning contact had been made with German armoured cars at Sidi Nisr – only fifty miles from either Bizerta or Tunis. Further north, 36th Brigade had advanced through Bône and over the border to Tabarka on the coast, and on 17 November leading units clashed with a German armoured column at Djebel Abiod; at the same time a link was established between these northern troops and the paratroopers in the centre at Sidi Nisr. Further south units from the 11th Brigade advanced along the Medjerda valley towards Medjez el Bab at the gateway of the Tunisian plain. Anderson was closing the ring.

But now the British general had to pause to concentrate for the attack on Tunis from the hills, and he reckoned a week would be needed to prepare for the assault. German reinforcements were rushing into Tunisia by the hour. Over to the east, Montgomery's forces had been held up by heavy rain from the 15th to 17th as they moved across the desert, and Rommel reached El Agheila on the

Opposite:
Surrealist landscape, after Pali. Painted by Rex Whistler.

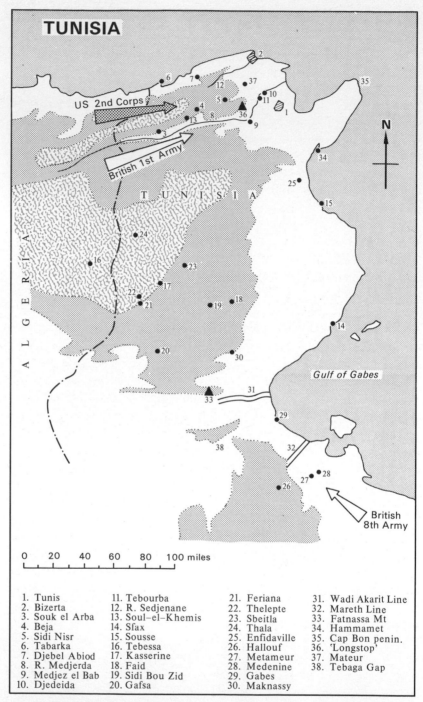

TUNISIA

US 2nd Corps

British 1st Army

T U N I S I A

A L G E R I A

N

Gulf of Gabes

British
8th Army

0	20	40	60	80	100 miles	

1. Tunis	11. Tebourba	21. Feriana	31. Wadi Akarit Line
2. Bizerta	12. R. Sedjenane	22. Thelepte	32. Mareth Line
3. Souk el Arba	13. Soul–el–Khemis	23. Sbeitla	33. Fatnassa Mt
4. Beja	14. Sfax	24. Thala	34. Hammamet
5. Sidi Nisr	15. Sousse	25. Enfidaville	35. Cap Bon penin.
6. Tabarka	16. Tebessa	26. Hallouf	36. 'Longstop'
7. Djebel Abiod	17. Kasserine	27. Metameur	37. Mateur
8. R. Medjerda	18. Faid	28. Medenine	38. Tebaga Gap
9. Medjez el Bab	19. Sidi Bou Zid	29. Gabes	
10. Djedeida	20. Gafsa	30. Maknassy	

23rd. 'Operations in Tunisia not going as fast as they should,' noted Brooke on the evening of the 23rd, 'and, on the other hand, Monty's pursuit of Rommel is badly delayed by weather. As a result Rommel given more time than I like to re-establish himself.' Next day the CIGS added: 'Am still very worried.' But Rommel was determined to withstand pressure to hold defensive positions at Agheila. 'I pointed out that fortifications, however strong, could not help us, as the enemy could outflank the whole line.' His critical petrol shortage meant that he would be unable to manoeuvre his troops south to prevent such a flanking movement; on 24 November Rommel therefore decided he must fly to East Prussia to plead with Hitler. He would arrive at the Führer's HQ on the 28th.

Anderson launched his thrust towards Tunis on the 25th. But German defenders reacted vigorously, and enemy positions blocked the 36th Brigade units in the north as they tried to push through the final pass from the Sedjenane valley. British and American troops further south had better success, capturing Medjez el Bab and reaching Djedeida airfield on the 26th – only ten miles from Tunis. Infantry rapidly followed up this armoured advance and forces were prepared for an assault on Djedeida itself. The attack began on 28 November, the same day that Rommel confronted Hitler. 'The *Afrika Korps* no longer matters,' shouted the Führer. The army must fight to the death; Rommel's pleas only resulted in an even more violent outburst. 'Go!' screamed Hitler. 'I have other things to do than talk to you.' Rommel saluted, clicked his heels, and made for the door. Hitler came running after him, put his arm round the Field-Marshal's shoulder and said: 'You must excuse me. I'm in a very nervous state. But everything is going to be all right.' Rommel returned to North Africa, convinced that the Führer must be insane and that only destruction awaited him in the desert.

But the advance on Tunis from the west had faltered. Anderson's attempts to take Djedeida between 28 and 30 November failed in the face of a fanatical defence, with the Germans scratching together an armoured group armed with the new Tiger tanks – armour which Rommel dearly needed over in the east. British and American casualties soared in the vicinity of Djedeida: by the 29th the 11th Brigade had only one company left fit to fight, and this suffered almost complete annihilation during the day. Allied forces clustered in the olive-groves and on the scattered hills, and tried frantically to reorganise, but the Axis defenders could concentrate quicker: a vicious counter-attack took place on 1 December. By 3 December the British and American troops were beginning to pull back, behind Tebourba. And now the rainy season began; according to Anderson 'its effect on the roads, on cross-country movements and on the airfields came as a very unpleasant

Troops of the 1/6
Queens Regiment
march into Tobruk.

Sunken ships in Benghazi harbour, battered by enemy artillery and air action and rendered increasingly untenable for the British in January 1942. Painted by Edward Bawden.

surprise ... Rain, mist and a peculiarly glutinous mud formed the background to all our operations during this period.' Troops shivered in their drenched outposts and struggled to bring up supplies from base ports far to the rear, while reinforcements poured in to the enemy defences from harbours and airfields just fifteen miles away.

With the 'Torch' forces increasingly bogged down in the west, only continued success by the 8th Army in the east could boost morale and retain allied initiative. And now Montgomery's forces moved towards El Agheila, scene of terrible fighting earlier in the desert war. 'As we approached the Agheila position I sensed a feeling of anxiety in the ranks of the 8th Army,' wrote Montgomery. 'Many had been there twice already; and twice Rommel had debouched when he was ready and had driven them back.' But after his disastrous visit to Hitler the Desert Fox had realised he must retire once a token defence had been made: regardless of orders he would pull back at the moment when the 8th Army attack seemed imminent, and as early as 6 December, when only the 8th Army's forward patrols were in the area, he had begun to

166

filter back his unmotorised Italian units. Montgomery originally intended to launch his main attack on the 15th but soon realised that the enemy had started to withdraw to defensive positions at Beurat, and he advanced the timing of the offensive. Heavy raids would be made on the main defences by 51st Highlanders, starting on the night of the 11th and aimed at pinning down Rommel's formations; the full attack would commence on the 14th. Meanwhile the New Zealand Division would carry out a 200-mile envelopment.

But the preliminary raids by the Highlanders proved unwise. These, with the supporting British artillery fire, convinced Rommel that the main offensive was about to begin, and he ordered full retreat.

> The British commander's planning had contained one mistake [he wrote later]. Experience must have told him that there was a good chance that we would not accept battle ... He should not, therefore, have started bombarding our strong-points and attacking our line until his outflanking force had completed its move.

The New Zealanders received urgent orders to increase their pace, 167 but ran into fuel difficulties and became increasingly stretched. The fleeing Germans streaked through the gaps; as Freyberg reported: 'Enemy in small columns including tanks passed through at high speed ... Most difficult to intercept ... Majority escaped round our flanks.'

The so-called battle of El Agheila resulted in 450 enemy prisoners being taken, plus twenty-five guns and eighteen tanks, while Rommel withdrew rapidly to the west relying on small but determined rear-guard actions and mines to slow his pursuers.

> I realised we were in the middle of a concentration of anti-personnel mines [wrote Major Samwell of the Argylls]. A cold shiver ran down my spine as I realised I had not only walked right through it, but had walked about in it. It was a nightmare of a struggle back ... I had to find out how far the mines extended ... No one except myself knew where they were, so there was nothing for it but to double back across the mined area myself. Crossing my fingers for luck I started back ... and arrived safely at the platoon ... Once more I had to face that nightmare journey back. The problem was whether to crawl slowly feeling for mine-prongs, or just to dash across and trust to luck. I decided on the second alternative, and bounded across, keeping as much as possible to the same route as before ...

Dogged pursuit continued, but still without immediate prospect of decisive battle. A victorious decision also eluded Anderson in the west. By 24 December the general believed he had gathered sufficient strength for another major assault forward for Tunis, and engineers had worked night and day to improve and widen roads and bridges for the latest heavy tanks to move up. But the rain had continued to swamp the area. Eisenhower visited Anderson's HQ – having had to travel by road since bad weather prohibited flying – and went with the British General to Soul-el-Khemis, HQ of the main attacking force, the British 5th Corps.

> The rain fell constantly [wrote Eisenhower]. I observed an incident which, as much as anything else, I think, convinced me of the hopelessness of an attack. About thirty feet off the road, in a field that appeared to be covered with winter wheat, a motor-cycle had become stuck in the mud. Four soldiers were struggling to extricate it but in spite of their most strenuous efforts succeeded only in getting themselves mired into the sticky clay ... We went back to headquarters and I directed that the attack be indefinitely postponed. It was a bitter decision.

Eisenhower reported to the Anglo-American Combined Chiefs of Staff in Washington that a resumption of the offensive would have to be delayed until better weather, which would be 'not less than two months ... Evidence is complete, in my opinion, that any
attempt to make a major attack under current conditions in

The symbolic end of Mussolini. A portrait of Il Duce lying in the mud of his African Empire, trodden on by the feet of his victorious enemies.

Northern Tunisia would be merely to court disaster.' Also on 24 December, General Alexander signalled from Cairo that although the port of Benghazi was discharging 1,900 tons of supplies a day, upon which the 8th Army depended for its continued being, this figure must be considered unreliable in view of the winter weather. The warning proved correct, and the tired 8th Army remained stationary before Beurat. In both east and west the allied advance had come to a halt.

Added to these military upsets came another shock on Christmas Eve: Admiral Darlan, upon whom the allies relied for French co-operation in North Africa, was assassinated in Algiers. Immediate dangers arose of civil disorder: Eisenhower, informed of the news while at Anderson's HQ, rushed back to Algiers. Now someone had to be selected to take up the mantle of French leadership: choice rested upon de Gaulle or Giraud, respectively favourites in London and Washington. The question would be added to the agenda at a forthcoming momentous meeting between Churchill and President Roosevelt, scheduled to take place at Casablanca in mid-January. And by then, divisions of opinion had arisen between

169

Tank crews make the most of a temporary halt in the pursuit. Behind them wait their 'General Grant' tanks.

the Americans and the British over Eisenhower's handling of military affairs in North Africa. Brooke had always held doubts over Eisenhower's appointment; he wrote later: 'It must be remembered that Eisenhower had never even commanded a battalion in action when he found himself commanding a group of armies in North Africa. No wonder he was at a loss.'

On 28 December the War Cabinet in London discussed the 'Torch' commander's performance, with this section of the top-secret minutes afterwards headed: 'No Circulation', Churchill referred to Eisenhower's decision to postpone the Tunis attack and added:

> In the meantime the enemy was continuing to reinforce his forces in Tunisia, which might also be reinforced by the bulk of Rommel's army from Tripolitania ... There were indications in General Eisenhower's telegram that matters were not running too smoothly between ourselves and the Americans ... Furthermore, units were being split up.

Next day, 29 December, Eisenhower explained his immediate policy to the Combined Chiefs of Staff: he intended to follow an 'aggressive defensive' in Northern Tunisia, using mainly British forces, and to launch an offensive further south towards Sfax with American troops, taking advantage of the easier terrain. He himself would take charge. Brooke and his colleagues in London felt even greater alarm: the Sfax operation might not only reduce the weight of the main attack in north Tunisia, further delaying the fall of Tunis, but it would also 'expose the northern forces to risk of defeat'. The Sfax scheme seemed to increase possibilities of a German counter-thrust from the north and a move by Rommel from Tripolitania; the British Chiefs of Staff also declared: 'We are much alarmed at the idea of Eisenhower leaving the centre and summit where he alone can cope with Giraud and make sure the front is properly supplied.' Eisenhower's plans would also be discussed at the Casablanca Conference in January.

The dramatic year ended with hopes deflated for a rapid, crushing victory in Tunis either from west or east. Brigadier Ian Jacob, of Ismay's staff, who had just visited the Tunisian front, supported Eisenhower's assessment in a report given to the British Chiefs of Staff on 4 January: rains would prevent operations in the north until the advent of spring weather. In the east, the 8th Army would begin to push onwards again at an earlier date, but a signal from Alexander on 5 January warned that 'administrative situation of 8th Army makes it impossible for its main body to move forward before night 14/15 January'. Yet despite these setbacks, allied arguments and the danger of loss of confidence, the scent of victory still remained and the climax of the battle for North Africa lay ahead.

Chapter 7

Roads to Tunis

Winston Churchill strode on the windy North African beach, paddling in the Casablanca foam and admiring the mighty rollers crashing in from the Atlantic – the same surf which had plagued 'Torch' landings three months before. Ten hours earlier, as the Prime Minister's aircraft had droned across the Mediterranean, Montgomery had issued a stirring message to his troops. 'The leading units of 8th Army are now only about 200 miles from Tripoli ... *The 8th Army is going to Tripoli* ... Nothing has stopped us since the Battle of Alamein began on 23 October 1942. Nothing will stop us now.' The advance against Rommel's position at Beurat would begin in three days' time, on the 15th, with a two-fisted attack by 30th Corps. Meanwhile Churchill, Brooke and the British delegation at the Casablanca Conference began their summit talks with Roosevelt and the American service chiefs; long hours would be spent trying to hammer out a common strategic policy for the next stages of the war.

Montgomery's attack began on schedule on the 15th. Against some seven hundred British tanks, Rommel could only scrape together ninety-one – two-thirds of them Italian. And once again the Axis army pulled back; this time Tripoli lay open to the allied advance, and the 8th Army rolled forward. At Casablanca, Eisenhower reported to the Combined Chiefs of Staff on the 15th and repeated his plans for an attack on Sfax, due to start in only nine days' time: Eisenhower claimed he was 'faced with the dilemma of either allowing the troops in the north [of Tunisia] to deteriorate by remaining inactive in the mud, or suffering some losses to them through keeping them more active. In his opinion the latter was the less of two evils.' Brooke remained unconvinced, and the subject received further attention next morning, 16 January, with the conference also attended by Alexander. Rommel's forces were still falling back before the 8th Army, and Alexander believed Tripoli would be taken within eleven days. But the Cairo commander added that no further advance in the east would be possible until Tripoli port had been cleared, and this might take many weeks; Rommel would thus be given breathing space in which to react against the American move on Sfax in the west.

Brooke stressed that the allied attacks would be in danger of being dealt with and defeated in detail – and, at last, he secured an agreement from Eisenhower that the Sfax offensive would be postponed until it could be linked with a renewed advance by the 8th Army from the east. After more discussion, sometimes heated, the

Opposite Crusader tanks push on from El Hamma.

173

The Prime Minister and
his Chiefs of Staff during
the Casablanca
Conference. Left to
right: Air Chief Marshal
Sir Charles Portal,
Admiral Sir Dudley
Pound, Mr Churchill in
RAF uniform, General
Sir Alan Brooke and
Lord Louis
Mountbatten.

Casablanca Conference also agreed on other even more important matters, including top-priority being maintained in the Mediterranean, rather than down-grading this theatre as secondary to a cross-Channel attempt against north-west Europe. The Combined Chiefs of Staff settled the delicate question of the command system in North Africa after the junction of the 8th and 1st Armies from east and west: the conference agreed to appoint Eisenhower as Supreme Commander, with Alexander his Deputy, while Tedder would be Supreme Air Commander. Brooke's doubts over Eisenhower's military abilities were therefore softened by the promised presence of Alexander by the American's side; moreover Eisenhower, as Supreme Commander, would deal primarily with political and inter-allied matters, rather than day-to-day military decisions. Even the thorny problem of French leadership received some kind of temporary solution: Charles de Gaulle had very reluctantly flown out to Casablanca to meet Giraud, and while a firm system of leadership had still to be worked out between these two rivals, at least it seemed they would work together for the moment.

174

'Tripoli, the 8th Army's ultimate objective for so many years, has fallen,' scribbled Private Crimp in his diary late on 23 January, the day the city was captured. 'The chase is still going in full blast, and Tunisia lies open.' But Crimp, squatting in the shade of his dusty, battered infantry truck, added:

> There, however, up north, things don't look so good. The British 1st Army and the Americans (green troops, I suppose), after struggling desperately all through the winter, are now tied down in the mountains. Jerry, on the other hand, having saved Tunis and pushing out a tough defence of the city, is said to be actually bringing large reinforcements over from Italy. (Doesn't the bastard know when he's bloody well whacked?)

Rommel, in fact, now prepared to take the offensive.

Meanwhile, as Rommel completed his plans for a last audacious bid for the initiative, optimism surged in London. Churchill took two hours to make a statement to Parliament on Thursday, 11 February. 'I thought I had a good tale to tell,' he commented in his memoirs. The highlight of his speech proved to be his quotation of a signal from Alexander, which declared: 'The orders you gave me on 10 August 1942 have been fulfilled. His Majesty's enemies, together with their impedimenta, have been completely eliminated from Egypt, Cyrenaica, Libya and Tripolitania. I now await your further instructions.' Members of Parliament cheered these historic words from the normally reticent British Middle East Commander:

A Bofors gunner on the alert in the harbour at Tripoli after the capture of the Port on 23 January 1943. The ship in the background has been torpedoed, but stayed afloat.

A British Tank Hunting Squad creeps into the foothills to prepare an ambush position.

in fact Alexander and Churchill had composed the telegram together during the Prime Minister's recent Mediterranean visit.

Axis troops opposite the 8th Army were now positioned in the old French frontier defences at Mareth, designed originally to cover Tunisia against an Italian attack from Tripolitania. This line stretched eighty miles from the Mediterranean to the Matmata hills and offered reasonable protection. Rommel could temporarily thin his forces for use elsewhere, and he also relied upon obtaining extra time through Montgomery's need to bring up supplies. He commented: 'Montgomery had an absolute mania for always bringing up adequate reserves behind his back and risking as little

176

as possible.' While these resources were being gathered by the British, and while his own troops were relatively secure, the Desert Fox planned to strike against the British and American forces on the other side of Tunisia, and then to switch back to lash out at his 8th Army tormentors.

For the attack west he could either send forces along the coastal strip, via Sfax and Sousse, or he could attempt a more dangerous thrust inland through the mountains. Rommel chose the latter: the unexpected advance might provide valuable surprise – and the allies would be hit in the rear, in the Tebessa area where forces were assembling for a resumption of the Anglo-American offensive. The plan reflected all Rommel's daring and opportunism. But he had to contend with more than numerically superior enemy forces: he had also to deal with divisions of opinion in the German High Command – between himself, von Arnim, who commanded the 5th Panzer Army in north Tunisia, and Field-Marshal Kesselring, C-in-C South. On 9 February Kesselring flew over from Italy to confer with the two subordinates: Rommel sought the boldest possible operation aimed at Tebessa via the mountains leading to Kasserine pass; von Arnim advised more caution and advocated a limited offensive designed to manoeuvre the Americans into a withdrawal. The conference resulted in a compromise: von Arnim in the north would advance through the Faid pass aiming at Sidi Bou Zid, while Rommel followed the line Gafsa–Feriana–Kasserine.

The twin offensives began with startling success. Early on 14 February von Arnim thrust from the Faid pass; Rommel's units entered Gafsa on the 15th. By the 17th Rommel was in Feriana and had taken the important airfield at Thelepte further north; von Arnim's 5th Panzers had taken Sidi Bou Zid and Sbeitla. Inexperienced American troops in the north had fallen back in confusion, so far losing 2,866 prisoners, 169 tanks and sixty-three guns. The German panzers seemed unstoppable as they whined along the narrow mountain roads. Heinz Schmidt, a company commander in Rommel's army, described the fast-flowing advance.

> I was rounding a sharp curve when I sighted and recognised a Sherman tank on the road ahead, within attacking range. I jerked the wheel in the driver's hand and the vehicle swerved sharply towards the bank of the road. The detachment manning the gun immediately behind me were swift in taking their cue. In a matter of seconds they had jumped from their seats, unlimbered, swung round and fired their first shell, while the Americans still stood immobile, the muzzle of the tank gun pointing at a hillock half-right from us. Our first shell struck the tank at an angle in the flank. The tank burst into flames. We probed ahead and soon ran into fire from tanks and machine-guns deployed on either side of the road . . . Steady fighting went on for an hour. Then thick columns of black smoke rose ahead, followed by explosions, obviously an ammunition dump. The enemy tanks ceased firing. We continued to advance . . .

Eisenhower rushed to the front, where he experienced increasing alarm. 'Realising . . . that reinforcements in men and equipment would be needed quickly and urgently, I hastened back to HQ to hurry them forward. We scraped the barrel . . .' Alexander hurried over from Cairo to become Eisenhower's deputy on 19 February, and next day appealed to Montgomery for help. But despite Montgomery's later assertions, any pressure by 8th Army to relieve the strain on the British and Americans in the west could have had little

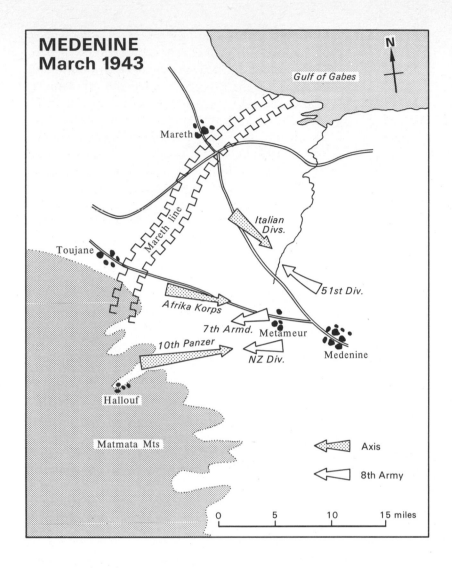

MEDENINE
March 1943

N

Gulf of Gabes

Mareth

Mareth line

Italian
Divs.

Toujane

51st Div.

Afrika Korps

7th Armd. Metameur

10th Panzer

NZ Div.

Medenine

Hallouf

Matmata Mts

Axis

8th Army

0   5   10   15 miles

practical effect: by now the Axis attack had already begun to break down, mainly through lack of unity between Rommel and von Arnim. The latter remained lukewarm over chances of total success, and failed to give Rommel vital support for the offensive launched by the latter against the Kasserine pass on the 19th and 20th.

By 5 p.m. on the 20th Rommel's panzers had broken through the pass, but the *Afrika Korps* units were now largely unsupported and the Americans were beginning to recover. 'Valuable time was being squandered,' wrote Rommel. 'I was extremely angry and ordered 179 the commanders to take themselves closer to the front where they could get a proper view of the situation.' He overcame his own exhaustion to drive his units forward, and by the morning of the 21st his tanks were moving down the roads towards Thala. Ahead lay the British 26th Armoured Brigade: bound by bound these British defenders had to pull back throughout the day, pressed by the 10th Panzer, until by early evening the British tanks were withdrawing through a thin line of infantrymen, a battalion of the Leicestershires, behind which only lay a fragile defensive screen of field and anti-tank batteries. Before darkness the infantry had also filtered through these guns and the latter stood alone. But the artillery somehow managed to hold throughout the night, and help arrived just in time. The artillery column of the 9th American Division, totalling forty-eight guns, which in four days had raced eight hundred miles from Morocco, drove into action straight off the line of march. And Rommel, still unsupported by Arnim, now only had about twenty-four hours' ammunition, six days' food and 120 miles of fuel per vehicle. At 1 p.m. on the 22nd he broke off the attack and his units limped back through the Kasserine pass.

Yet the situation remained perilous for the allies. On 26 February von Arnim advanced towards the British 5th Corps at the northern end of the 1st Army, and managed to pin down these units; Rommel was moving his units back to the east ready to strike against the 8th Army. Alexander sent a depressing signal to Churchill on the 27th: 'I am frankly shocked at whole situation as I found it . . . Hate to disappoint you, but final victory in North Africa is not just around the corner.'

Rommel prepared to rush against the British in the east, hoping Montgomery's forces had been unsettled by the need to make premature moves to help the Americans in the Kasserine struggle; indeed, at the end of February the British commander told his Chief of Staff that he 'now found himself unbalanced'. But the Desert Fox had no faith in the proposed attack; he himself now wanted to fall back to better defensive positions at Enfidaville. His superiors in Rome and Berlin remained adamant. Arguments amongst the Axis high command led to disastrous delay, and Montgomery's Chief of Staff reported that 'by 5 March we were ready'. Rommel's attack began next day. He planned an advance by 10th Panzer from Hallouf on the New Zealand and 7th Armoured positions between Metameur and Medenine, supported by an *Afrika Korps* thrust on the left – yet his units would drive directly into a carefully prepared British defence. The 30th Corps was responsible for holding the 8th Army front, and the regiments were well dug into

excellent emplacements, with 350 field and medium guns, 460 anti-tank guns, 300 tanks and ample ammunition; the British units enjoyed brilliant support from the Desert Air Force. Rommel suffered no delusions: 'An attack against the 8th Army at Medenine was bound to be an extremely difficult undertaking.' Panzers filed past their leader on the evening of the 5th as they moved to their assembly points: Rommel, standing in his open car, was described by one eye-witness as 'obviously a sick man', suffering from jaundice and with a dirty bandage wrapped round desert sores on his neck.

Fog shrouded the enemy movements at dawn on the 6th, but clashes with 8th Army forward patrols at the foot of the Matmata hills revealed Rommel's intentions. Shelling began at about 6 a.m. The first enemy tanks to be seen came from the Toujane–Medenine road, swinging north against the 7th Armoured Division, and as the mist dispersed German guns could be seen taking up positions further back. The 8th Army's artillery remained silent, obeying orders not to fire prematurely. The leading line of tanks halted about a mile and a half from the 7th Armoured defences and British officers could see the German tank commanders sweeping the countryside with their field glasses. After a few moments they seemed to have made up their minds: turrets slammed shut and the tanks squealed forward again; they reached the boundary of a dummy minefield and then, as hoped, swung towards rising ground. At last the British guns began to open fire at these easy targets: two six-pounders from the 73rd Anti-Tank Regiment began by knocking out four Mark III Specials at 4,000 yards range, and mortars

Troops wait behind the stone walls for the German tanks to advance upon the well-defended British positions at Medenine. Italian mines, lifted from the road, have been placed nearby.

181

from the 28th Maori Battalion blew the tracks off a fifth and worried it until it burst into flames. Machine guns slaughtered the enemy crews as they baled out.

Hour after hour the same story was repeated throughout the day, and mounds of burning, spluttering tank hulks marked the line where the futile German assaults washed against the rigid 8th Army defences.

> The rumbling they made was terrific and it gradually got nearer and nearer [wrote the historian of the Scots Guards, describing the advance of 21st Panzer]. Then quite suddenly three of them appeared peeping over the ridge. They were obviously suspicious, rather like a little party of deer, but as they could see nothing they came lumbering on. We let them just get over the crest and then every gun opened up and in ten seconds all three were on fire.

Infantry fared no better; Major Samwell in the Argylls gave this description of an attempted enemy assault.

> They were a mixed bag of Germans in their khaki uniform of the Afrika Korps and Italians in their dark green tunics. They advanced by sections in close formation, and offered an admirable target. I took over a Bren gun myself, and, shouting to the others to hold their fire, waited until they were within four hundred yards; then I gave the signal, and we let them have magazine after magazine. All along the front we could hear the Brens and rifles cracking. Then enemy sections stopped, wavered, broke into a double, and pushed on, stopped again, and finally dived for shelter among some scattered olive trees. They must have suffered terrible casualties.

To the south-east in the 5th New Zealand Brigade area, the climax came at 5.45 p.m. At intervals from 3.30 p.m. onwards advancing infantry of 10th Panzer had been dispersed by fire from the Divisional artillery without coming to grips with the New Zealand infantry, and now the Germans made one last attempt. Forward observation posts reported back that 'something special was coming up'. About a thousand German infantry formed up in three waves, accompanied by strong clusters of tanks and supported by artillery; almost immediately after the advance began these attackers found themselves subjected to a devastating concentration from New Zealand artillery fire and the whole enemy line seemed a mass of thudding, gushing explosions. The attack was smashed before it even got properly started, and the forward troops never even obtained a target for their rifles. 'When the area was inspected after the battle,' reported the official New Zealand historian, 'it was found that there was rarely more than six yards between the fall of shot.' By last light the battle had finished. British patrols pushed forward into the Matmata foothills during the night and experienced only minimum contact with the enemy. By dawn on the 7th the Axis army had gone. 'At first light a wonderful sight was revealed,' wrote Major R. C. G. Foster of the Queen's Royal Regiment. 'Within a few hundred yards of the Queen's Brigade positions the ground was littered with disabled and abandoned tanks and vehicles, twenty-seven tanks on the 1/7th Battalion's front alone.'

> Attack after attack was launched but achieved no success [commented Rommel]. It soon became clear that the attack had failed and there was nothing more to be done about it ... The attack had bogged down in the break-in stage and the action never had a chance of becoming fluid. The British commander had grouped his forces extremely well ... In fact the attack had been launched about a week too late ... A great gloom settled over us all. The 8th Army's attack was now imminent and we had to face it. For the Army Group to remain in Africa was now plain suicide.

Rommel quit North Africa on 9 March. He had 'finally decided to fly once again to the Führer's HQ. I felt it my duty to do all in my power to rouse a true understanding of the practical operational problems of Tunisia.' He confronted Hitler again on 10 March, without success: Africa must be held. Rommel himself would not witness the final destruction of his beloved *Afrika Korps*. Hitler ordered him to go on sick leave and refused to listen to the Field-Marshal's request to go back for just a few more days. In North Africa, von Arnim took over for the last struggle.

Arnim decided on 11 March that his forces would not withdraw from the Mareth line. He felt confident in the strength provided by these old French defensive positions; to the north lay the sea and to the south protection would be provided by the stark Matmata mountains, which stretched westwards to the apparently impassable Dahar sand wilderness. But Montgomery had discovered chinks in the enemy shield. Back in December he had sent forward the Long Range Desert Group on a reconnaissance operation, and this mission had located a gap through the mountains from Foum Tatahouine; Montgomery now planned to despatch a force through this gap, along the edge of the Dahar, and then through the vital Tebaga Pass in the north which would open a way to the plain of El Hamma and Gabes – behind the enemy at the Mareth line. This left hook would consist of a New Zealand Corps under Freyberg, amounting to about 25,000 men and 150 tanks, stiffened by the 8th Armoured Brigade, an armoured car regiment, extra artillery and a Free French column. Meanwhile 30th Corps was to deliver the main attack against the eastern flank of the Mareth line

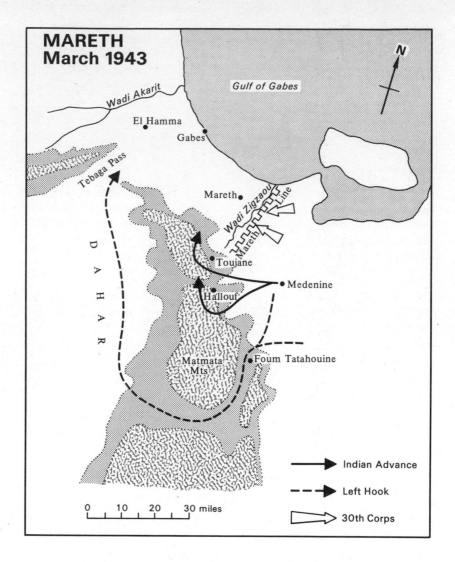

**MARETH
March 1943**

Wadi Akarit

Gulf of Gabes

El Hamma

Gabes

Tebaga Pass

Mareth

Wadi Zigzaou

Mareth Line

D A H A R

Toujane

Medenine

Hallouf

Matmata
Mts

Foum Tatahouine

0   10   20   30 miles

→ Indian Advance

--→ Left Hook

⇨ 30th Corps

proper; breaking in, rolling it up from east and north, and advancing towards Gabes. This offensive would begin on the night of the 20th, after having allowed time for the New Zealand hook to slip through the mountains and into position at Tebaga. It seems clear that Montgomery originally conceived the main blow by 30th Corps to be the primary means whereby the enemy would be destroyed, rather than through the New Zealand outflanking movement: the course of the battle compelled him to change his mind.

Freyberg's force started to assemble at Foum Tatahouine during the night of the 11th/12th. On 16 March units of 30th Corps started preliminary assaults on outposts of the Mareth line, as a diversion from the New Zealanders and as a preparation for the main offensive. By the 19th the left hook had cleared the mountains and had begun to move round the edge of the Dahar, and it reached the positions before Tebaga next morning. By now, 20 March, the enemy had discovered the whereabouts of this New Zealand threat, and Montgomery ordered the abandonment of all further concealment attempts – Freyberg's units must 'go like hell'. At the same time began the main offensive by 30th Corps against the east of the Mareth line itself, and on the night of the 20th an attempt was made by the 50th Division to secure a bridgehead across anti-tank ditches in the Wadi Zigzaou – a vital advance if British armour were to strike into the enemy defences. Penetration by the infantry units was achieved during the night, but vigorous enemy counter-attacks limited the advance and the Wadi had still to be bridged for tank passage; at 11.30 a.m. on the 21st Montgomery reported to Alexander that the enemy clearly intended to fight with all his strength. 'I am preparing a dog-fight in Mareth area which may last several days.' During the day the 30th Corps HQ ordered the 50th Division to complete its attack during the night of the 21st, and to ensure 'without fail' that one crossing place over the Wadi Zigzaou was completed of the three that were being attempted.

The attack went in soon after dark amidst a thick hail of artillery, mortar and machine-gun bursts. Infantry clawed forward, and behind them ran divisional engineers to build suitable tracks for the tanks: working against time and suffering heavy casualties these engineers completed a causeway soon after midnight, and in the early hours of the 22nd, forty-two Valentines managed to cross. Forward infantry cheered the welcome sound of revving tank engines as this slender armoured force emerged from the Wadi behind them, lumbering on in a north-westerly direction. But the British tanks soon encountered mines and anti-tank guns, and this armoured advance had so damaged the causeway across the Wadi that further repairs had to be carried out before reinforcements could trickle through. Desperate fighting continued on the morning of the 22nd, and by noon the engineers had completed the necessary strengthening. Then came a sudden, swamping cloud-burst which wrecked the causeway and stranded the troops in the bridgehead.

Without ammunition, and without anti-tank guns, with communications failing, the units in the bridgehead seemed in no position to withstand a determined enemy counter-attack. This began at 1.40 p.m., launched by 15th Panzer towards the section of the bridgehead held by the Durham Light Infantry. First the more powerful German tanks picked off the British Valentines which had 185

Major-General B. C.
Freyberg, Commander
of the New Zealand
Corps.

crossed the Wadi the previous night: the Germans sat back out of
range of the British guns, and one after another the Valentines were
hit and burst into flames; by 5 p.m. only about fifteen British tanks
remained and these scuttled to better cover near the Wadi crossing.

The enemy proceeded to attack each Durham Light Infantry
post in turn with infantry and with tanks giving close support from
hull-down positions. Miraculously, the British line continued to
hold, despite acute shortages of ammunition and despite the total
lack of anti-tank weapons. Panzers pressed in and managed to

thrust between the DLI positions; another determined attack would have meant inevitable destruction of the ragged defenders. 'Instead they shouted to the men of 8th DLI ... to surrender,' wrote the regiment's historian, 'saying that the position was hopeless. This invitation was replied to by more Bren and rifle fire.' The pockets managed to hang on until nightfall, and reinforcements struggled across the Wadi to the forward line. But the situation remained desperate, and the 30th Corps commander, Leese, expressed his fears to Montgomery at a 2 a.m. conference on the 23rd.

'Leese was very upset,' wrote Montgomery. 'I said: "Never mind, this is where we've got 'em; but you *must* keep the German reserves tied to your Corps front."' The 8th Army commander nevertheless altered his plans: the main blow would be shifted from the British right to the left hook at Tebaga. The 30th Corps would continue to engage the enemy as much as possible, and the 4th Indian Division would attempt to force a way through the mountains, while the principal effort would be made by Freyberg's New Zealanders which had so far made no progress at Tebaga, but which would now be reinforced by 10th Corps armoured units under Horrocks.

These reinforcements reached the New Zealanders on the afternoon of the 26th; Montgomery had ordered a combined air, tank and infantry assault to be made before dark and almost within minutes this had begun.

> Punctually at 3.30 p.m. the fighter-bombers appeared [wrote Brigadier H. K. Kippenberger], squadron after squadron: all along the line of the forward infantry little columns of orange smoke appeared indicating their positions, and this smoke steadily grew and spread ... Very soon there were several columns of black smoke from burning trucks or tanks. The whole narrow area between the hills looked like a cauldron.

His eye-witness account continued:

> Under cover of the noise and smoke of this bombardment, in clouds of dust, the Sherman tanks of the Notts Yeomanry and Staffordshire Yeomanry rumbled up, passed on either side of Hill 201 and deployed along the infantry start-line ... At 4.15 p.m. the tanks moved majestically forward, followed closely by our little carriers. The infantry climbed out of their pits – where there had been nothing visible there were now hundreds of men, who shook out into lines and followed on five hundred yards behind the tanks. At 4.23 p.m. the barrage lifted a hundred yards – an extraordinarily level line of bursting shells – tanks and infantry closed to it and the assault was on.

By midnight British armour had broken the enemy defences and had rumbled through the gap. German panzers turned and began to flee, and an extraordinary spectacle occurred in the pale moonlight as opposing tanks raced one another through the dust to the vital village of El Hamma. The Germans reached these defences first and their commander, von Liebenstein, threw up a thin line of field artillery and anti-tank guns to block the British advance. He gained valuable time to prevent an 8th Army encircling movement behind the Mareth line, and once again the *Afrika Korps* slipped away – this time to Wadi Akarit. Men of the 8th Army, weary, filthy, but triumphant, moved forward again. Churchill and Brooke celebrated with a sumptuous supper in the drawing room at Ten Downing Street: plovers' eggs, chicken broth, chicken pie, chocolate soufflé, all eased down with champagne, port and brandy.

Allied forces from west and east were now converging. On 17 March Patton's 2nd US Corps had begun its advance through Gafsa to the north-east of Arnim's forces, and had taken Maknassy on the 21st to threaten the German rear; on 24 March, even before the push through the Tebaga Gap, von Arnim had urged his superiors that withdrawal should begin in view of the American threat and the 8th Army outflanking offensive. By the end of the month British units in the 5th Corps, in north Tunisia, ended a four-week slogging match by restoring the position in the coastal sector, and Patton's armour had renewed the thrust down the Gafsa–Gabes road – thereby imposing a northern threat on the enemy's positions at Wadi Akarit and causing the despatch of 10th Panzer to halt this advance. Ahead lay yet another Axis defensive line, this time commanded by the Italian General, Messe. Zero hour for the 8th Army attack would be the night of 4/5 April.

On the 3rd, General Alexander issued his orders for the final campaign in Tunisia, co-ordinating the efforts of both the 1st Army in the west and 8th Army in the east. First would be the 8th Army's task of driving the enemy from the Gabes Gap at Wadi Akarit, with Montgomery assisted by flanking pressure from Patton's 2nd Corps. The 8th Army would then be able to advance into the coastal plain, where its superior armour and motorised formations could be used to best advantage, while the 2nd Corps would be transferred to the extreme north on the left of the 1st Army. The 8th Army would strike north towards Sousse and Enfidaville.

Montgomery held a conference with his commanders to outline his plan for the Wadi Akarit attack: this amounted to a frontal assault by the 51st Division, with the 10th Corps driving through the subsequent hole, while the 4th Indian Division moved forward on the left to the lower ground beneath the dominating and apparently unassailable Fatnassa mountain. Tuker, commander of the 4th Indian, voiced objections: he believed the 51st Division would suffer heavy casualties, and he added that a way might conceivably be found for his 4th Indian Division to scale Fatnassa in a surprise night attack, thus moving round to secure a powerful bridgehead for the 10th Corps. Montgomery agreed to the attempt, and at the same time reinforced the attack to be made by the 51st Division by adding units of the 50th.

'This present week the general battle in Tunisia will begin,' signalled Churchill to Stalin on the 7th. It had already begun, at 4 a.m., as Tuker's troops filtered forward on Fatnassa. The operation provided a perfect opportunity for the Gurkhas to display their grim skills in close-quarter combat as they crept upwards in the pitch-black from ridge to ridge. German defenders were hacked down as they tried to stem this ghastly, silent assault; by dawn a gap had been prised in the enemy defences. Tuker told Horrocks at 8.45 a.m. on the 7th that 'the way was clear for 10th Corps to go through … Immediate offensive action would finish the campaign in North Africa.' But over on the right of the British front the advancing formations from the 51st Division had run into deadly German defences, suffering heavy casualties, and the setback gave the enemy the opportunity to retreat once more. Montgomery could nevertheless claim another victory: 'My troops are in TREMENDOUS form', he cabled to Churchill. And also on the 7th, advancing 8th Army units linked with troops from Patton's 2nd Corps: forces coming from Alamein in the east thus met Americans landed in 'Torch' in the west. 'Hello Limeys!' shouted the dust-covered GIs, regardless of the fact that the troops they greeted were Indians. Sfax fell to the advancing allies on the 10th; on 12 April the town of Sousse was seized, and about a thousand prisoners were now being rounded up each day by the 8th Army. Also on the 12th the Italian-German forces opposing Montgomery were almost established in their last bastion – Enfidaville.

But now the 8th Army, so long victorious, seemed about to shift to the side-lines. Despite Montgomery's eagerness – and confident expectation – to lead his forces forward for the final destruction of the enemy in North Africa, Alexander realised that this offensive on Tunis must be based primarily on the attempts by the 1st Army in the good tank country further inland and further north. Before Montgomery lay the difficult Tunisian mountains; the Medjerda valley and the easier terrain in the 1st Army area formed the natural gateway to Tunis and Bizerta.

Alexander therefore sent a disappointing signal to Montgomery on the evening of the 12th: 'Main effort in next phase of operations

Victory. Citizens of
Tunis cheer a Churchill
tank and its triumphant
crew.

will be by 1st Army. Preparations already well advanced for attack; earliest date 22 April. Most suitable area for employment of armour is in the plain west of Tunis.' The 8th Army GOC was asked to supply strength for this offensive. 'Require 1 Armd. Div and 1 Armd. Car Regt to join 9 Corps from you as early as can be arranged.' Alexander added: 'Hope you can develop maximum pressure possible against Enfidaville position to fit in with 1st Army attack ...' This directive to exert pressure rather than attempting to inflict total defeat clearly relegated the 8th Army to a subsidiary role, and seemed a recognition of the fact that the enemy positions at Enfidaville – where Rommel had long since wanted defences to be taken up – would be far stronger than any encountered by the 8th Army since Alamein: attempts to assault the Germans in this rugged country would lead to terrible casualties.

Yet Alexander modified his orders, either through Montgomery's enthusiasm or through indications that opposition to the 1st Army would be stiffer than previously expected. On 16 April he sent Montgomery new instructions: now the 8th Army would continue to push forward 'by an advance on the axis Enfidaville–Hammamet–Tunis' to prevent the enemy from withdrawing into the Cap Bon peninsula. 'All my troops are in first class form,' declared Montgomery, 'and want to be in the final Dunkirk.' And on the night of the 19th his forces were thrown forward at the fierce mountain slopes above Enfidaville, despite fears expressed by Horrocks and others that 'we will break through, but I doubt whether at the end there will be very much left of the 8th Army'. Montgomery dismissed the fears: the enemy would be 'bounced' from their defences.

This time the Germans and Italians refused to withdraw. Rarely in the North African campaign did the fighting prove to be so savage.

> In the darkness men grappled and slew each other [declared a historian of the Indian Division]. The survivors went to earth as bombs burst about them, rose and rushed forward in the dust and smoke and fastened upon enemies ... Every gain drew a counter-attack from desperate men pledged to hold the heights at all costs. Yard by yard the assailants worked upwards, around rocky knolls, across mountain wadis, surging over crests to face other crests from which mortar and small arms fire swept down incessantly upon them ...

Bodies lay heaped around the German positions, and by dawn less than three miles had been gained. Throughout 20 April both sides clung to the hills, while the 50th Division made slow progress up the coastal plain. Even Montgomery realised the attempt must be

192

temporarily halted – a fresh attack would be sent in on the 25th.

Meanwhile the 1st Army launched its offensive on the 22nd. The 9th Corps in the centre, reinforced by the 1st Armoured Division from the 8th Army, managed to make a penetration yet failed to achieve a breakthrough; further north the 5th Corps renewed the struggle for the twin peaks of 'Longstop' – Djebel el Ahmera and El Rhaa – over which the Coldstream Guards, the US 18th Infantry, and the Germans had fought for control since before Christmas. Possession of this feature was vital in any advance from Medjez towards Tebourba, and by darkness on the 22nd the first crest had been gained by the allies, but neighbouring peaks remained in enemy hands. Further north still, the 2nd US Corps was making slow progress against difficult positions in the valley of the Sedjenane and in the tangled hills before Mateur. The opening of the offensive by the 1st Army therefore failed to achieve dramatic success – and Montgomery still believed the opportunity remained for his 8th Army to win the race to Tunis. He condemned the 1st Army assault as 'more of a partridge drive than an attack' and completed his plans for the renewed attempt on the Enfidaville positions.

He flew off to Cairo on the 25th to voice complaints over preparations for the invasion of Sicily, to take place after North Africa had been cleared; that night his troops resumed their dreadful climb up to the German defences; over the rocks they crawled, from one deep-dug enemy trench to another.

> I crept up [wrote Gurkha Jemadur Dewar Singh] and found myself looking into the face of a German ... He was fumbling with his weapon so I cut off his head with my *kukri*. Another appeared from a slit trench and I cut him down too. I was able to do the same to two others, but one made a great deal of noise, which raised the alarm ... I was now involved in a struggle with a number of Germans, and eventually after my hands had become cut and slippery with blood, they managed to wrest my *kukri* from me ... They then beat me to the ground where I lay pretending to be dead. The Germans got back into their trenches ... My platoon advanced and started to hurl grenades among the enemy ... I managed to get to my feet, and ran towards my platoon.

The defenders proved as brave as the attackers; once again dawn broke with the Germans still secure in their positions.

> Men have begun drifting back in small groups, [wrote Private Crimp] most of them badly shaken. They talk of crawling up sheer precipices to find every level expanse swept by machine-gun fire; of wounded rolling all the way down to the bottom; of trip-wires, mines and booby-traps on handgrip ledges ... and of walls and caves and all sorts of cunning defensive devices on the summit, piled round with the dead of previous assaults.

193

Both the 8th and 1st Armies had found the way virtually blocked.
Latest military reports were discussed by the War Cabinet in
London on the 27th, and in reply to a question by Churchill,
Brooke said he 'would inquire why General Montgomery had found
it necessary to go to Cairo at this juncture'. Montgomery was in fact
back in Tunisia, having returned from Egypt the previous day –
only to retire to his bed in his famous caravan, suffering from 'flu
and tonsillitis. Next day, 28 April, Alexander reported that Montgomery's forces were 'undoubtedly tired, and the 4th Indian
Division and the 7th Armoured Division are the only veteran ones
which can be considered from now onwards as capable of full
offensive action'.

These two divisions, plus the 201st Guards Brigade, were now
chosen to reinforce the 1st Army in the west for the renewed thrust
on Tunis. The decision, reached independently and almost
simultaneously by both Alexander and Montgomery, proved a
perfect solution to the problem of which armies and formations
should be represented at the final battle. The 7th Armoured and

4th Indian had taken part in Wavell's first desert campaign in December 1940, and the 201st Guards, then known as the 22nd Guards Brigade, had joined the Western Desert Force far back in April 1941. The Desert Rats would be there for the kill. The offensive would be launched on 6 May, with Anderson striking with overwhelming strength along the road from Medjez el Bab. Meanwhile the 2nd US Corps had continued to battle through the hills in the north and by 30 April at last threatened to encircle the Germans in the Sedjenane valley: the enemy pulled back, but now Bizerta lay within reach of the American corps, and General Omar Bradley, who had taken over command from Patton, prepared to assault alongside the British on the 6th.

Only hours remained before the death or capture of those grimy, bewildered yet brave Germans and Italians who still survived behind the battered defences, and who had been ordered by Hitler to fight to the end. On 27 April von Arnim had reported his troops were nearing total exhaustion; next day he had described his fuel situation as 'catastrophic'. About 135,000 German and 200,000 Italian soldiers stood ready for the onslaught. And, on 6 May as scheduled, the 1st Army launched the final blow, with the offensive entrusted to the 9th Corps now under General Horrocks from the 8th Army.

In the early hours of the morning the infantry divisions advanced to their objectives behind a massive rolling artillery bombardment, reinforced by heavy bombing when daylight came, and by 9 a.m. the way had been cleared for armour to pass through. The Germans and Italians continued to fight, often to the last man, and by dusk the British tanks still remained fifteen miles from Tunis. But opposition at last began to crumble; next morning, 7 May, the tanks moved on relatively unhindered and British forces entered the outskirts of Tunis. Leading armoured cars of the 6th and 7th Armoured Divisions, the Derbyshire Yeomanry and the 11th Hussars, reached the centre of the city in the afternoon – and the 11th Hussars had been the first unit to cross the frontier wire into Libya when the Italians declared war in June 1940. American tanks entered Bizerta at about the same time, and by the morning of the 8th both centres had been completely subdued. By noon on 9 May the Axis army in the northern sector had laid down weapons before the Americans, and after further operations in the last army refuge, the Cap Bon peninsula, von Arnim surrendered the *Afrika Korps* on the 12th. Also on this Wednesday Messe accepted unconditional surrender for all remaining Axis forces in Tunisia.

A last message had flashed from North Africa to the German

High Command. 'Ammunition shot off. Arms and equipment destroyed. In accordance with orders received German *Afrika Korps* has fought itself to the condition where it can fight no more. The German *Afrika Korps* must rise again ...' The wires fell silent. An equally short signal reached Winston Churchill, then in Washington, at 2.15 p.m. on Thursday, 13 May. This time the terse phrasing better matched Alexander's character. 'Sir. It is my duty to report that the Tunisian campaign is over. All enemy resistance has ceased. We are masters of the North African shores.'

Over 238,240 prisoners had been taken. About 620,000 enemy troops had been killed or captured during the North African campaign; British losses totalled 220,000, with the majority belonging to the 8th Army.

> For most of them [wrote a Desert Rat officer, Captain Sean Fielding] there is a grave in the sand, perhaps a few rocks piled over them, their names in a hurried pencil-scrawl upon a cross made of petrol cases. For some there is no cross: only a mound of sand that the wind will soon soften and gently erase.

Aftermath. 'For some there is no cross,' wrote an 8th Army officer, 'only a mound of sand that the wind will soon soften and gently erase ...'

Select Bibliography

Alexander, Field-Marshal the Earl: *The Alexander Memoirs*, London, 1962.

Barnett, Correlli: *The Desert Generals*, London, 1960.

Bryant, Arthur: *The Turn of the Tide, 1939–1943*, (study based on Lord Alanbrooke's diary and notes) London, 1957.

Carver, Michael: *El Alamein*, London, 1962.

Carver, Michael: *Tobruk*, London, 1964.

Churchill, Sir Winston: *The Second World War*, Vol. II, *Their Finest Hour*, London, 1949; Vol. III, *The Grand Alliance*, London, 1950.

Connell, John: *Auchinleck*, London, 1959.

Connell, John: *Wavell, Soldier and Scholar*, London, 1964.

Crimp, R. L.: *The Diary of a Desert Rat*, London, 1971.

Crisp, Robert: *Brazen Chariots*, London, 1959.

de Guingand, Major-General Sir Francis: *Operation Victory*, London, 1963.

Eisenhower, Dwight D.: *Crusade in Europe*, London, 1948.

Haupt, Werner, & Bingham, J. K. W.: *North African Campaign*, London, 1968.

Kippenberger, Major-General Sir Howard: *Infantry Brigadier*, Oxford, 1949.

Lewin, Ronald: *Montgomery as Military Commander*, London, 1971.

Lewin, Ronald: *Rommel as Military Commander*, London, 1968.

Macksey, Kenneth: *Crucible of Power*, London, 1969.

Montgomery, Field-Marshal the Viscount: *Memoirs*, London, 1958.

Parkinson, Roger: *Blood, Toil, Tears & Sweat*, London, 1973.

Parkinson, Roger: *A Day's March Nearer Home*, London, 1974.

Playfair, Major-General I. S. O.: Official War History, U.K. Military Series, Campaigns; *Mediterranean and Middle East*, Vols I–IV, London, 1962–66.

Samwell, Major H. P.: *An Infantry Officer with the 8th Army*, London, 1945.

Schmidt, Heinz: *With Rommel in the Desert*, London, 1951.

Strawson, John: *The Battle for North Africa*, London, 1969.

Tedder, Lord: *With Prejudice*, London, 1966.

von Mellenthin, Major-General: *Panzer Battles, 1939–1945*, London, 1955.

Young, Desmond: *Rommel*, London, 1950.

Index